From Biscuits to Lane Cake

Emma Rylander Lane's

Some Good Things to Eat

FOOD *and the* AMERICAN *South*

From Biscuits to Lane Cake

Emma Rylander Lane's

Some Good Things to Eat

Edited by

Evan A. Kutzler

MERCER UNIVERSITY PRESS

MACON, GEORGIA

2023

MUP/ P676

© 2023 by Mercer University Press
Published by Mercer University Press
1501 Mercer University Drive
Macon, Georgia 31207

27 26 25 24 23   5 4 3 2 1

Books published by Mercer University Press are printed on acid-free
paper that meets the requirements of the American National
Standard for Information Sciences—Permanence of Paper for Printed
Library Materials.

Printed and bound in the United States.

This book is set in Adobe Garamond and American Typewriter.

Cover/jacket design by Burt&Burt.

ISBN   978-0-88146-902-8
Cataloging-in-Publication Data is available from the
Library of Congress

For Evelyn, with love.

MERCER UNIVERSITY PRESS

Endowed by

TOM WATSON BROWN
and
THE WATSON-BROWN FOUNDATION, INC.

Contents

Foreword

"Do not raise a family without making tea or ginger cakes for the children once a week. Otherwise, you rob childhood of one of its rights, also one of its chief joys."

Emma Rylander Lane published those words in 1898, at the dawn of the age of domestic science in America. The movement, which was to take hold in the nation's public schools, would eventually be renamed home economics and then be recast again and again, as family and consumer sciences, or as applied human sciences. Its foundation was the belief that caring for the home was among the noblest of professions. Keeping house well, its adherents believed, was a worthy subject to be taught in the high schools, in the newly developing teacher education institutions called normal schools, and in more established colleges and universities.

Emma Rylander Lane's *Some Good Things to Eat*, the only book she would ever write, is more than a kitchen "how-to." She equated domesticity with virtue. She understood that a well-crafted recipe, fully realized as an elegant salad or a stately cake, was a means to bring joy into the household, particularly in her native South in the years following the devastation of the Civil War. Her book was eminently practical, instructing its readers about the subtleties of baking a cake in the summer as opposed to the procedures to be followed in winter. Yet that practicality led to something more: the realization that good cooking led to good living.

It was a profound book, at a cost of fifty cents. And it was a technical wonder. Each recipe, Emma tells the reader, was "carefully tested." One of the recipes has kept her name alive in the annals of Southern culinary history ever since—a cake that this humble librarian agreed to name for herself, she writes, only at the insistence of a friend, after it captured first place in a county fair competition in Georgia. In 2016, the Lane cake was voted the Official State Dessert of Alabama by the legislature. Harper Lee mentions the cake twice in *To Kill a Mockingbird.*

Two years after Emma published her cookbook, she was drawing upwards of 75 students to her Columbus, Georgia, cooking classes, where she greeted enrollees with tastes of deviled ham. Emma introduced her readers and her students to the newest gadgets of the age, grinding that ham in a hand-cranked mill that could be affixed to a kitchen counter and touting the virtues of wondrous innovations such as crabmeat out of a can.

Upon her death in a small Mexican village in April of 1904, however, the book she had researched so thoroughly and written so lovingly was not even mentioned in her obituary, published by her hometown newspaper, the *Americus Times-Recorder.*

The only known original copy of her book is in the Patrick Cather Collection at Auburn University.

Enter Evan Kutzler and the book you are now reading. A talented public historian with strong ties to former President Jimmy Carter and former First Lady Rosalynn Carter, Evan has undertaken the resurrection of this underestimated collection. As he points out, even though the Lane cake has been Emma's posthumous calling card, her book represents far more.

If a Lane cake seems too laborious, readers can easily follow Emma's detailed instructions for beaten biscuits, cheese wafers, pound cake, or seven different varieties of deep-fried croquettes. In fact, I am inspired to chop some chipped beef, soak it in boiling water, drain it well, and slather it in mayonnaise for Emma's Emergency Salad. I might even take her advice for embellishment: chopped boiled eggs, celery seed, and mustard seed. This republished volume reminds us that dishes just taste better when we know something about their history.

Fred Sauceman
Series Editor

Introduction

Family, Food, and Questions:
Searching for Emma Rylander Lane

A light dusting of snow fell on Buena Vista in Marion County, Georgia, in the last week of January 1863. "The house tops, fences, trees and everything save the bare wet ground is white with snow," Ann Mathis Rylander wrote. "The pendant icicles from the eaves of the houses are such as we very seldom see this far south." The winter scene made Ann worry about her husband, John "Emory" Rylander, a major in the 10th Georgia Infantry Battalion stationed in Virginia. Yet the snow at her parents' home, where she spent part of the war, offered great entertainment for her three children: Emma, Carrie, and Arthur. "The children are in great glee over the snow," Ann continued. "All of them have their hands full. Arthur wanted his cooked, and Emma puts it in the coals to try and is laughing one of her hearty laughs as he keeps telling her 'it is all cooking up!'"[1] Thirty-five years later, Emma Rylander Lane dedicated

---

[1] Ann Rylander to "My Dear Emory," January 28, 1863, John Emory Rylander Papers, 1855–1863, Stuart A. Rose Manuscript, Archives, and Rare Book Library, Emory University. In 1852, John Dinkins Mathis's family lived in Georgia Militia District 710 in western Marion County. In 1860, his household appears near Buena

Some Good Things to Eat to her mother, "whose early training developed in me a love for the culinary art," as well as her husband, Davis Lane, "whose discriminating and appreciative appetite has been my inspiration." In the clearest childhood description of the future notable cook, Emma was already showing her passion for cooking.

Emma Rylander Lane was the culinary artist behind the "Lane cake," a popular Southern cake in the twentieth century. After the Lane cake appeared in *Some Good Things to Eat* (1898), different versions of the recipe began to appear. Attributed to a different Lane, one recipe appeared in *Atlanta Woman's Club Cook Book* (1921). The Lane cake later appeared in Henrietta Stanley Dull's revised *Southern Cooking* (1941). By the time Jean Louise "Scout" Finch ate a piece of "Lane cake so loaded with shinny it made me tight" in *To Kill a Mockingbird* (1960), it was already a well-known Southern cake that required a wineglass of whiskey to make its icing.[2]

The culinary artist, though, fell into obscurity as her cake's popularity rose. Aside from *Some Good Things to Eat*, only a few newspaper articles clearly contain Emma's voice. Her

---

Vista. Georgia Tax Digests, Marion County, 1852, Georgia Archives, 68.

[2] Meredith Bethune, "What Ever Happened to the Boozy Cake in 'To Kill a Mockingbird'?" *NPR*, July 15, 2015; Tori Avey, "American Cakes—Lane Cake," November 11, 2014 (last updated April 24, 2022), https://toriavey.com/toris-kitchen/lane-cake-history-recipe/; Harper Lee, *To Kill a Mockingbird* (New York: Grand Central Publishing, 2010 [1960]), 171; Mrs. S. R. Dull, *Southern Cooking* (Athens: University of Georgia Press, 2016 [1941]), 247. The Lane cake was the only cake recipe added to the 1941 edition.

sudden death in Mexico, combined with scholarly inattention to women's history for most of the twentieth century, put the cake and the woman it was named for on separate tracks. While one cannot fully recover the intricacies of her life, there is value in the search for Emma Rylander Lane. First, her southwest Georgia roots and lifelong connections to the region raise questions about Alabama's official state dessert. It is at least as likely that the cake originated in the pooled knowledge of southwest Georgia and as that of southeast Alabama cooks. A fuller accounting of Lane's life, alongside a reprint of *Some Good Things to Eat*, also reveals that she was more important to Southern cooking than a single cake.

Childhood Rumors and Traumas

At six and a half years old in January 1863, Emma was the oldest child of Emory and Ann Mathis Rylander. She was born one year after her father graduated from Emory College in Oxford, Georgia, and just ten months after her parents married. Emory was a bookish man who spent his final months in college searching for his fiancée's approval in love letters instead of studying for his philosophy and astronomy courses. "Not a day, nay I not safely say an hour, rolls over me but it brings some serious thoughts of the past or future," Emory told Ann in March 1855. "And strange to say I invariably link the future, with all of its enjoyments and pleasures, with you." Emory laid out his hopes for a happy life, his concerns that Ann would sacrifice too much for his comfort, and his desire to amass "a good library" in their future home. Five months later, they married in Marion County.[3] After Emma came a second daughter, Carrie, in March 1859. When the census enumerator came to the Rylander house in Americus in September 1860, Ann was expecting her third child, Arthur, who was born two months later.[4]

Americus was a small but growing city and an important economic hub for southwest Georgia. Charles W. Hancock, a printer from South Carolina who started the city's first successful newspaper, documented the changes wrought by the railroad. "Contractors and operators are all astir," the *Sumter Republican* noted. "The country is already enlivened by grading and excavations, and before many months will have [passed], the people will rejoice at the sound of the whistle and the rattling of the car." The sounds of progress reached a crescendo in September. Hancock wrote, "The mechanic is to be seen busily plying the instruments of his profession, and every breeze wafts to the ear the hum of industry and enterprise." When the first steam locomotives arrived in October 1854, the sounds of an emerging city replaced the "crack of the rifle" and

---

[3] Marriage Book A, 1844–1866, Marion County Courthouse, Buena Vista, Georgia; Stephen W. Berry II, *All That Makes a Man: Love and Ambition in the Civil War South* (Oxford University Press, 2003).

[4] 1860 US Census, Sumter County, Georgia, 27th District, population schedule, pg. 469, dwelling 804, family 810, J. E. Rylander, A. E. Rylander, Emma Rylander, Carrie Rylander; digital image, Ancestry.com, accessed September 21, 2021; citing NARA microfilm publication M653, roll 136.

"the sounds of a woodman's axe" that once dominated the courthouse town.[5] The tastes of Americus, like the sound of the rifle that brought down game, also changed in the 1850s. While staples like cornmeal and pork remained the center of Southern eating for several more generations, the railroad brought greater variety to the plain fare. In 1856, Fred Vogelgsang promoted his bakery as having "the finest French Pastry and Ornamental Cakes." Another German baker opened a confectionary and fruit store in 1855 and advertised "Brandies, Wines, Cordials, Syrups, Nuts" as well as "pastry and ornamental cakes." In 1860, Isham Harvey ran a butcher shop, and the 1869 city directory listed a butcher, a confectionary, an icehouse, restaurants, and more than a dozen grocers.[6]

While the city had no public schools until the Reconstruction era, a number of private academies served white children. Emma's parents ran a private academy at the corner of College and Elm Streets. Her grandfather, Matthew Edmund Rylander, had connections to Wesleyan College in Macon,

---

[5] Evan Kutzler, "Listening to Early Americus," *Americus* (GA) *Times-Recorder*, August 15, 2019; Evan Kutzler, "Oak Grove Cemetery: A Shelter for the Dead, A Park for the Living," *Americus* (GA) *Times-Recorder*, October 22, 2020.

[6] *South-Western News* (Americus, GA), August 6, 1856, Newspaper #1437, Rubenstein Library, Duke University; 1860 US Census, Sumter County, GA, 27th District, population schedule, pg. 443, dwelling 619, family 626, Isham Harvey; digital image, Ancestry.com, accessed September 21, 2021; citing NARA microfilm publication M653, roll 136; *Americus City Directory* (publisher not identified, August 1869.)

Georgia. Moving from Macon to southwest Georgia in the 1850s, Matthew Rylander established a Methodist school at Magnolia Springs west of the Plains of Dura (now just Plains). Her grandfather's Sumter County house, built about 1850, was the center of a large plantation.[7]

FIGURES 1,2 Emma was both a child of the Confederacy and of a specific part of the South that escaped much of the war's up-close destruction. While there were food shortages elsewhere, including bread riots, the planter class in southwest Georgia had plenty of provisions in 1864 and 1865. When Matthew Rylander wrote his will in March 1864, one month after the first prisoners arrived twenty miles away at Andersonville, he directed "six mules or horses, twelve head of cattle, and one hundred head of hogs and all my sheep" to his wife "from among my stock." He also bequeathed to his wife "one yoke of steers" and "a sufficiency of corn, wheat, potatoes, & peas, [and] oats for the support of herself and Negroes for one year after the division of my property."[8] That fall, a planter from the other side of the county slaughtered 50,400 pounds of pork. About 5,500 pounds of the meat went to the Confederate government.[9]

The Civil War hurt the Rylander family in other ways. In 1864, two days before Emma's eighth birthday, news of Emory

[7] Elizabeth Barthold, "Matthew Edmund Rylander House" (Jimmy Carter Interim House), Historic American Building Survey, summer 1989, https://www.loc.gov/pictures/item/ga0576/.

[8] Matthew E. Rylander Will, 1864, Probate Records, Sumter County Courthouse, Americus, GA.

[9] John B. Lamar Plantation Book, Hargrett Library, UGA, n.p.

Rylander's death arrived. He had been killed in his unit's first major battle. Some said the bullet at Cold Harbor seemed to just fall out of the sky. It was a random event and only one other man in the unit was slightly wounded that day. "He was much beloved by his Regiment, and had he lived, he would have risen to distinction," the *Sumter Republican* asserted. "He was the son of our esteemed fellow citizen M. E. Rylander of this county, with whom, and the stricken family, our community sympathize in their bereavement." A month later, the newspaper printed the grisly details: the fatal bullet, "a stray ball from the enemy's skirmishers," struck Emory "behind the right ear and passed entirely through the back of the head."[10]

The circumstances of his death, including the apparent randomness of it all, spurred rumors that compounded the family's grief. Despite the public accolades, Major Rylander had a mixed reputation among enemies and friends. His battalion guarded Camp Oglethorpe, a prison for US soldiers in Macon, for most of 1862. Fredrick F. Kiner, a chaplain in the 14th Iowa Infantry and a prisoner of war, described Emory as "cruel and tyrannical," and he asserted that Major Rylander "was hated both by us and his own men, many of whom censured him as much as we did." For Kiner, the officer

---

[10] The first mention of his death indicates that word arrived the previous Saturday evening—too late for the last Saturday's news. "Maj. J. E. Rylander," *Sumter Republican*, June 11, 1864; "For the Sumter Republican," *Sumter Republican*, July 16, 1864. See also William J. Moseley, 10th Ga. Infantry Battalion Civil War Miscellany, Personal Papers, Microfilm Drawer 283, Reel 35, Georgia Archives.

symbolized the aristocratic despotism of Southern slavery under which common soldiers were not far above the level of slaves.[11]

Emory may have, to some extent, agreed with the comparison of army life to slavery. In the spring of 1861, just after joining the army, he lamented the orders that prevented him from exploring Staunton, Virginia. "Military discipline is absolute, and no freeman can consent to live under it, but for the Good of his country," he wrote. "We are just beginning to know what slaves soldiers are." The distance and discipline made him yearn for home. While walking at sunset that same day, Emory reflected on his family in southwest Georgia. "Could I but see them once more," he wrote, "and spend the remainder of my days in loving affection!"[12]

The army made Emory reflect on his readiness to die and his hope to be a better father and husband and man if he lived. He wanted to be buried in Georgia so that his family could visit him and his wife might one day lay alongside him. The war also compounded Emory's loneliness and, at times, alienation from his loved ones. "Feel sad and neglected this morning," he wrote in July 1861. "The mail has come, and still no letter from

---

[11] F. F. Kiner, One Year's Soldiering, Embracing the Battles of Fort Donelson and Shiloh, and the Capture of Two Hundred Officers and Men of the Fourteenth Iowa Infantry, and their Confinement Six Months and a Half in Rebel Prisons (Lancaster, PA: E. H. Printer, 1863), 121–23; Stephen Hoy and William Smith, *Camp Oglethorpe: Macon's Unknown Civil War Camp, 1862–1864* (Macon, GA: Mercer University Press, 2019), 25, 34–36, 39.

[12] John Emory Rylander Diary, July 7–8, 1861, unpublished family collection.

home. I wonder if I am forgotten, it seems so. Others hear from home, from relatives, and friends, I hear from No-one." Full of self-pity, he concluded, "If my family ever gets this, they may know that I feel worse this morning than I choose to put in my diary." Again and again, he remarked on the inconsistency of letters from home and used his two 1861 diaries, "prepared for Mrs. Ann E. Rylander," as a form of extended communication with (or, rather, at) his wife to ease his loneliness.[13]

When orders came for Rylander's battalion, stationed in Macon for most of 1862, to return to Virginia that fall, it probably marked the last time the family saw their father and husband alive. The birth of a fourth child, Walter, in January 1863 suggests that he visited home on furlough while his unit guarded prisoners. This also may have been the subtext behind Emory's protests against returning to Virginia that, on the surface, had to do with his men's sickness and climate. His battalion had 570 men in November 1862, but only 191 soldiers were well enough for duty. "We are from Southern Georgia, unaccustomed to the rigor of a Northern winter; and to be so suddenly moved into snow and ice would I fear prostrate the entire command," Emory argued, and he proposed instead moving to defend Charleston or Savannah.[14]

---

[13] Rylander Diary, July 8, July 18, August 3, 1861. See also Rylander Diary, preface, August 14, and August 26, 1861.

[14] John Emory Rylander to Adjutant General S. Cooper, November 17, 1862, and John Emory Rylander to Gen. Thomas Jordan, November 9, 1862, "Letters Received by the Confederate Adjutant and Inspector General, 1861–1865," M474, Record Group 109, War Department Collection of Confederate Records, National Archives and Records Administration, Washington, DC. The birth

The request failed, and the battalion struggled to reacclimate in the Army of Northern Virginia. Future Georgia governor Henry Dickerson McDaniel described the taunting to his future wife, Hester C. Felker, who lived near Emory's alma mater. "Did you ever chance to hear mention of the Rylanders?" he asked. "This is the soubriquet of a Battalion in our Brigade. Those fellows were guards in Macon and are not by any means the cream of the arms-bearing population." Most could not keep up with the march through the muddy roads. "Every straggler from any Regiment of the Division was shouted at as a Rylander," McDaniel reported. "Poor fellows! Their initiation into active campaigning was rather too severe."[15] Emory chafed at the nicknames "Laplander," "Lowlander," and "Greenlander" hurled at him by soldiers in other regiments until he complained to Gen. George T. Anderson. "The Major went away," a letter to the *Savannah Republican* reported, "looking like he wished he had not made a complaint."[16] The battalion's assignment—prison duty in Richmond—signaled that their reputation did not rise. Some wondered aloud whether one of Emory's own men had shot him as they maneuvered into position at Cold Harbor.

---

of Walter Rylander (1863–1882) comes from his headstone, Oak Grove Cemetery, Americus, GA.

[15] *With Unabated Trust: Major Henry McDaniel's Love Letters from Confederate Battlefields as Treasured in Hester McDaniel's Bonnet Box*, ed. Anita B. Sams (Monroe, GA: Walton Press, 1977), 141.

[16] "Letter for Virginia," *Savannah* (GA) *Republican*, May 19, 1863.

The rumor was not a universal opinion. Evidence also existed that Emory's reputation among his own men rose before his death. Or perhaps the suspicious death erased the memory of these complaints. In his diary, William J. Moseley described the same details of Emory's fatal wound from a "stray ball" as the soldiers moved into position at dusk. "Oh, if Maj. Rylander was only alive," he wrote four months later. "No man could be more missed than he is in this Battalion. The men are not the same."[17] Francis Marion Coker directly sought to dispel the speculation that Emory's death was murder. "The rumor you mentioned about Rylander's death I think untrue—that he was killed by his own men," Coker told his wife. "He was with his command far in the rear and not engaged, but killed by what we call a 'stray shot.' It was either chance or fate. The men spoke highly of him. Their aversion, as is usual in such cases, had turned to like and preference, and they regret his death."[18] Whether chance or fate or murder, Emma lost her father in the late spring of 1864 under unusual circumstances—even for the Civil War years.

The family brought Emory home and buried him with his brother—Emma's uncle—who died near Richmond that same summer. Emma never wrote about the effects of losing her father or the rumors about murder. One wonders about the lasting effect. Despite being a child of the Confederacy, there is no

---

[17] William J. Moseley Diary, June 3, 1864 and September 20, 1864, Civil War Miscellany, Personal Papers, Microfilm Drawer 283, Reel 35, Georgia Archives.

[18] Francis Marion Coker to Sarah Alice Reid Coker, June 20, 1864, Francis Marion Coker Papers, MS15, Box 1, Folder 7, Hargrett Library, University of Georgia, Athens.

available evidence Emma joined the Daughters of the Confederacy in the decade before her death. She certainly did not use her public voice in *Some Good Things to Eat* to affix her commercial hopes to the Civil War memory or the Lost Cause. Was this intentional? Did she carry a different private memory of the war that conflicted with the dominant white Southern narrative at the time? Her father was publicly lauded as a hero, but did the rumors cast a shadow over his family and children?

The Rylander family recovered, at least financially, from the war. In 1860, Emory reported $2,400 in real estate (mostly land and buildings) and $4,000 in personal property (mostly enslaved people).[19] A decade later, Ann's personal wealth had fallen to $1,500 with the end of slavery, but her real estate had increased to $7,000. Fourteen-year-old Emma attended school, almost certainly the Furlow Masonic Female College, where her mother taught as a teacher in the primary department.[20]

---

[19] 1860 US Census, Sumter County, GA, 27th District, population schedule, pg. 469, dwelling 804, family 810, J. E. Rylander; digital image Ancestry.com, accessed September 21, 2021; citing NARA microfilm publication M653, 136.

[20] "Reminiscences of the Furlow Masonic College: A Paper Read by Mrs. Charles M. Williams before the Literary Club," *Americus* (GA) *Times-Recorder*, March 11, 1913; 1870 US Census, Americus, Sumter County, GA, dwelling 643, family 631, pg. 318A (stamped), Anne E. Rylander; digital image, Ancestry.com, accessed June 6, 2021; citing NARA microfilm publication M593, roll 174; Alan Anderson, *Remembering Americus, Georgia: Essays on Southern Life* (Charleston, SC: History Press, 2006).

[**Figures 3,4**] The Furlow Masonic Female College, founded in 1860 as a private school for children of a wide age range, closed during the Civil War but reopened soon afterwards. Emma Rylander was likely present when Sidney Lanier gave a commencement address on June 30, 1869, rebuking the rising public role of women during the Civil War era. "I am afraid, because yonder in Europe, yonder in the North, I hear certain deluded sisters of yours crying aloud that women must vote, that women must hold political office, that women must be lawyers and physicians and ministers," he told listeners. "But listen. On that instant, when this cause shall have attained its accursed objection, on that instant the prophetic agony of Othello's tortured soul will consummate itself in a million manly bosoms, on that instant we will love you not, on that instant chaos will come again." Lanier's message was clear: if women voted or became ministers, lawyers, or physicians, then men "could not love you, for you would be no whit different from men, and men do not love men." The fissures in Southern patriarchy that Lanier hoped to mend would eventually open wider in the form of women's literary organizations, publications, and greater public political activism.[21]

Emma followed in her educated parents' footsteps. In 1875, at age eighteen, she served as an assistant in the primary department while she and her sister Carrie continued their education. Both sisters took piano lessons. The commencement

---

[21] "Commencement Exercises of Furlow Masonic Female College," *Tri-Weekly Sumter Republican* (Americus, GA), June 22, 1867; Jay B. Hubbell, "A Commencement Address by Sidney Lanier," *Americus Literature* 2/4 (January 1931): 390 [385–404].

exercises recognized Carrie as the best student in "deportment" and Emma received honorable mention for drawing and painting. In 1878, Emma became the first librarian for the Americus Library Association. "It was a subscription library," an Americus resident remembered fifty years later, "but only a nominal fee entitled one to the use of the books and every year the directors put their hands in their pockets and paid the library out of debt."[22]

The Whole Household

When Emma looked back on her cooking experience about 1900, she calculated that she had twenty-five years of experience. Most of this overlapped with her marriage to Davis Thomas Lane. The two married in Sumter County in the fall of 1881 and had four children: Thomas (1882), Annie (1884), Carrie (1888), and Dave (1893).[23] Her book, *Some Good Things to Eat*, followed in the tradition of domestic manuals written by women and for women that helped define and negotiate the gendered expectations of the household. "The first thought of every woman when she assumes the duties of home should be her kitchen, as the health, happiness and prosperity

---

[22] "Their Defense," *Americus* (GA) *Times-Recorder*, July 7, 1921.

[23] Marriage Certificate, Rylander Vertical File, Lake Blackshear Regional Library, Americus, GA; 1900 US Census, Columbus, Ward 2, Muscogee County, GA, dwelling 109, family 123, pg. 6, Davis Lane, Emma R. Lane, Thomas Lane, Anna Lane, Carrie Lane, Dave Lane, Clifford Johnson, Ezekiel J. Bradley, Bennie Bradley, Ralph Bradley; digital images Ancestry.com, accessed June 6, 2021; citing NARA microfilm publication T9, roll 165.

of a family depend largely upon the character of the food eaten and upon the wisdom and economy of the housewife," she wrote. "All of you love sunshine and sugar, and if you value your husband's sweet temper you *must* give him his three daily meals well cooked and properly served."

[**Figures 5,6**] While Emma made no explicit mention of African American cooks in *Some Good Things to Eat*, her use of stock African American imagery in the original text and an advertisement in the *Clayton Record* offers a reminder of the multicultural roots of Southern cooking. "In coming before the public as an authority on cooking and all things pertaining thereto," Emma wrote, "I wish it clearly understood, that I am not a professional baker and have never been to a cooking school." This pointed to a practical origin of her expertise in the observation and management of African American men and women. "My knowledge of cooking is not theoretical, but thoroughly practical," she continued, "having been gained in my own family kitchen, with the use of plain, wood-burner cooking stoves, and my only help, such negro cooks as every housekeeper in the south has to contend with."[24]

This important acknowledgement placed Emma's recipes, including those in *Some Good Things to Eat*, within the race, class, and gender crossroads of Southern foodways. Emma wanted it known, though, that she had actually made the recipes herself. As she told prospective readers, "There are few dishes that I have not made with my own hands from the time

---

[24] Emma Rylander, [No Title], *The Clayton Record*, November 24, 1899.

honored 'hoe cake' of our grand-mothers, to the whitest, dain-tiest 'angel food' of the present day." Invoking her grandpar-ents' generation, Emma hinted at how the availability of wheat flour in the South changed culinary expectations. Her juxtapo-sition of hoecake, a food common among poor whites and en-slaved African Americans, to the "whitest" angel food reveals her understanding of how class and race divided eating experi-ences across society.[25] Until Emma turned nine years old, she was part of a slaveholding family. Her father's household con-tained a twenty-two-year-old enslaved woman and her two-year-old daughter. Ten miles away, Emma's paternal grandfa-ther's plantation included forty enslaved men, women, and children in 1860. This grandfather's estate also included an en-slaved couple in Bibb County who lived near—and might have worked for—Wesleyan College. Emma's maternal grandfather in Marion County also owned a plantation.[26] In freedom, Black

---

[25] Ibid. On cornbread, see Joe Gray Taylor, *Eating, Drinking, and Visiting in the South, an Informal History* (Baton Rouge and London: Louisiana State University Press, 1982), 83–84.

[26] 1860 US Census, Slave Schedules, District 16 and 27, Sum-ter County, GA, pg. 441 (stamped), J. E. Rylander; digital image, Ancestry.com, accessed May 21, 2022, M653, roll not identified; 1860 US Census, Slave Schedules, District 26, Sumter County, GA, pg. 451 (stamped) M. E. Rylander; digital image, Ancestry.com, ac-cessed May 21, 2022, M653, roll not identified; 1860 US Census, Slave Schedules, Macon, Bibb County, GA, pg. 95 (stamped), M. E. Rylander; digital image, Ancestry.com, accessed May 21, 2022, M653, roll not identified. Four years later, state tax digests suggest the enslaved woman had a second child. Georgia Tax Digests, Militia District 26, J. E. Rylander, Sumter County, GA, 1864, Georgia State Archives, Morrow, GA.

domestic servants remained in Southern kitchens. In 1900, the Lane household included seventeen-year-old Clifford Johnson, a female domestic servant who lived in a one-story house at the back of the property. For generations, race and cooking was a story of both change and continuity.[27]

African American Rylanders

Who were the African American Rylanders? In spring 1865, neither large armies nor emancipation had reached southwest Georgia. Emancipation came in the middle of the 1865 growing season before the last crops planted by enslaved people had ripened. Matthew Rylander mentioned several African American Rylanders in his 1864 will, including Meredith, who did not work in the fields and may have worked in the kitchen.

About half of the Rylanders who became free in 1865 stayed in Sumter County and retained the same last name. One household, adjacent to Matthew Rylander's house in western Sumter County, included two Minions, two Blakes, and an eleven-year-old Rosana Rylander who worked as a domestic servant. Abner and Melissa Rylander, their daughter Carolina, and three grandchildren—Jesse, Lavina, and William—also lived nearby. A few miles further away lived Mahala and Alexander Rylander with seven children or younger siblings. Walter

---

[27] 1900 US Census, Columbus, Ward 2, Muscogee County, GA, dwelling 109, family 123, pg. 6, Davis Lane, Emma R. Lane, Thomas Lane, Anna Lane, Carrie Lane, Dave Lane, Clifford Johnson, Ezekiel J. Bradley, Bennie Bradley, Ralph Bradley; Ancestry.com, accessed June 6, 2021; citing NARA microfilm publication T9, roll 165.

and Sallie Rylander, a young couple aged twenty-two and eighteen, lived in the southwestern part of the county, as did Betsey Rylander with her two sons, Nicholas and Frank. On the northern side of the county lived a cook named Matilda Rylander with her two small children, James and Thomas.[28]

Emma relied on African American labor, knowledge, and skills throughout her life. Acknowledging this fact is foundational for appreciating the significance of *Some Good Things to Eat*. After all, when she thanked "my friends who have so kindly contributed to this book," including many by name in Georgia and Alabama, she recognized this collaborative nature of culinary knowledge. "Contradiction is a central theme in the history of southern food," culinary historian Marcie Cohen Ferris writes, "where the grim reality of slavery, Jim Crow segregation, extreme hunger, and disfranchisement contrast with the pleasure and inventiveness of the region's cuisine."[29] Any

---

[28] 1870 US Census, Americus, Sumter County, GA, dwelling 989, 989, 865, 321, 311, 712, family 983, 984, 861, 314, 304, 707, pg. 375A, 335A, 335A, 249A, 248B, 356B (stamped), Doctor Minion, Eliza Minion, Allen Black, Charles Blake, Rosanna Rylander, Abner Rylander, Melissa Rylander, Caroline Rylander, Jesse Rylander, Lavina Rylander, William Rylander, Betsey Rylander, Nicholas Rylander, Frank Rylander, Mahala Rylander, Alexander Rylander, Jackson Rylander, Mary Rylander, Nancy Rylander, Henrietta Rylander, Frances Rylander, Ada Rylander, Walter Rylander, Sallie Rylander, Matilda Rylander, James Rylander, Thomas Rylander; digital images, Ancestry.com, accessed May 21, 2022; citing NARA microfilm publication M593, roll 174.

[29] Marcie Cohen Ferris, *The Edible South: The Power of Food and the Making of an American Region* (Chapel Hill: University of North Carolina Press, 2014), 1. On African American centrality to

effort to "preserve" Southern history in the twenty-first century, including the republication of an early cookbook, requires pushing beyond the traditional boundaries of historical imagination.

Some Good Things to Eat

Emma Rylander Lane earned regional notoriety for winning a baking contest in Columbus, Georgia, in the 1890s. "Plenty of Southern cooks have a version of the Lane cake in their repertoire, and some even claim to have originated it," John Egerton writes, "but the true creator was Emma Rylander Lane of Clayton, Alabama."[30] Egerton's work summarizes the dominant historical memory of the Lane cake. After a variety of Lane cakes emerged in the mid-twentieth century, Cecily Brownstone hoped to "set the record straight about one of the most famous cakes in American culinary history" in 1967 because the "cake has been attributed to others than its rightful creator, and its formula has often been desecrated."[31] Brownstone worked with

---

Southern cooking, see Jessica B. Harris, *High on the Hog: A Culinary Journey from Africa to America* (New York: Bloomsbury USA, 2011) and Kelly Fanto Deetz, *Bound to the Fire: How Virginia's Enslaved Cooks Helped Invent American Cuisine* (Lexington: University Press of Kentucky, 2017); John T. Edge, *The Potlikker Papers: A Food History of the Modern South* (New York: Penguin Books, 2017).

[30] John Egerton, *Southern Food: At Home, on the Road, in History* (Chapel Hill: University of North Carolina Press, 1993), 318–19; John T. Edge, *A Gracious Plenty: Recipes and Recollections from the American South* (New York: HP Books, 1999), 221.

[31] Cecily Brownstone, "Here's the Truth about the Lane Cake," *The Morning Herald* (Uniontown, PA), December 26, 1967.

her friend Emma Rylander Law, who had a copy of her grand-mother's scarce cookbook. Both Brownstone and Law republi-cized the Lane cake as it appeared in 1898. Law achieved her own notoriety as a cooking consultant and coauthored *Savannah Sampler Cookbook* and *Georgia Sampler Cookbook.*[32]

One Clayton tradition, preserved in Rebecca Parish Beasley's 1976 reprint of *Some Good Things to Eat*, contends that Emma baked the first Lane cake at the home of Joseph Edward and Lucy Walker Parish on Eufaula Street. "My grand-mother," Beasley writes, "was a neighbor and close friend of Mrs. Lane's. They experimented with foods and cooking ideas in the Parish home where I was reared."[33] Emma took the cake to the Columbus Fair, demonstrated her cooking for the Buck Range Company, but won first prize with the cake she had baked on the wood stove in Parish's kitchen. According to this account, the cake was baked there, rather than in the Lane kitchen, because the Parish house was more modern. A varia-tion on that tradition hints that Lucy Walker Parish, not Emma, came up with the recipe. At the very least, the two women shared recipes. Emma attributed the cheese wafer and mixed mustard recipes in *Some Good Things to Eat* to this

---

Newspapers reprinted similar articles around the country at about the same time.

[32] Margaret Wayt DeBolt and Emma Rylander Law, *Savannah Sampler Cookbook* (West Chester, PA: Whitford Press, 1978); Margaret Wayt DeBolt, Emma Rylander Law, and Carter Olive, *Georgia Sampler Cookbook* (Brookfield, MO: Donning, 1983).

[33] Rebecca Parish Kelly [Beasley], *Some Good Things to Eat* (Clayton, AL: Clayton Record, 1976).

friend. The lack of an attribution of the Lane cake to Lucy Parish suggests that Emma considered it her own recipe.[34]

[**Figure** 7] Brief and passing reference to "Emma Rylander Lane of Clayton Alabama" in the cake's history overlooks the mobility of the Lane household. These moves raise questions about Clayton as the intellectual origin of the cake. Davis Lane's job as a railroad telegraph operator kept the family moving from one place to another. All four Lane children were born in Georgia between 1882 and 1893, and Emma's real estate transactions show that she maintained her connections to Americus for all of the 1880s and 1890s.[35] In the mid-1890s, the family lived in Eufaula and Clayton for a few years before returning to Columbus by 1900. Four years later, the Lanes moved to Cananea, Mexico. It is impossible to know with certainty where Emma developed her cake, and she does not attribute the recipe to a specific friend in South Carolina, Georgia, or Alabama. Based on the available evidence, though, it is likely her recipe had roots in Georgia, where Emma lived almost her entire life.[36]

---

[34] Rebecca Beasley, phone conversation with author, May 27, 2022.

[35] Sumter County Deed Book W, pg. 795, 218, 350; Sumter County Deed Book X, pg. 2, 13; Sumter County Deed Book Z, pg. 512–13, 717; Sumter County Deed Book BB, pg. 227–28, 234–35; Sumter County Deed Book FF, pg. 360; Sumter County Courthouse, Americus, GA.

[36] 1900 US Census, Columbus, Ward 2, Muscogee County, GA, dwelling 109, family 123, pg. 6, Davis Lane, Emma R. Lane, Thomas Lane, Anna Lane, Carrie Lane, Dave Lane, Clifford

The publication of *Some Good Things to Eat* came at a specific moment in Southern women's history. The end of slavery transformed the relationships between Southern African American women and Southern white women. The increasing importance of white women in Southern political discourse that Sidney Lanier cautioned against in 1869 had grown into a cohesive political movement that sought to vindicate the South, something Southern men had been unable to accomplish during the Civil War. The United Daughters of the Confederacy, founded in 1894, experienced rapid growth in membership and political power over the next two decades. The organization placed monuments on city squares, curated papers in historical societies and "relics" for museums, and presided over the creation of textbooks that would influence the next generation of children.[37]

The rise of the United Daughters of the Confederacy coincided with the rise of Southern cookbooks. "Cookbooks bridge the era of Reconstruction to the early New South," Marcie Ferris argues, "when these seemingly benign texts became

---

Johnson, Ezekiel J. Bradley, Bennie Bradley, Ralph Bradley; Ancestry.com, accessed June 6, 2021; citing NARA microfilm publication T9, roll 165; *Walsh's Columbus, Georgia, City Directory* (Charleston, SC: Lucas & Richardson, 1900), 296; "Local Laconics," *Columbus* (GA) *Daily Enquirer*, December 16, 1899; "Personal Mention," *Columbus* (GA) *Daily Enquirer*, December 28, 1899; "Death of Mrs. Davis T. Lane, Former Americus Lady Died Sunday in Mexico," *Americus* (GA) *Times-Recorder*, April 26, 29, 1904.

[37] Karen L. Cox, *Dixie's Daughters: The United Daughters of the Confederacy and the Preservation of Confederate Culture* (Gainesville: University Press of Florida, 2003), 19.

increasingly important in a growing consumer culture and the selling of a remembered South to southerners, outsiders, and tourists."[38] As an educated Southern woman, an avid reader, and a food lover, Emma would have known about cookbooks that helped to inspire middle-class Southern housekeepers, including *Common Sense in the Household: A Manual of Practical Housewifery* (1871), *Mrs. Hill's Southern Practical Cookery and Receipt Book* (1872), or *The Dixie Cook-Book* (1885). These books wallowed in Southern post-emancipation frustrations, according to Harris, of "postwar depression, servant problems, and outdated kitchens."[39]

Emma's preface, in contrast, reads less like an attempt to vindicate her region or Southern womanhood and more like a practical guide for cooking in a changing world of improving railroads and grocery stores for middle-class households. "Only a limited number of recipes are here given, but all are known to be good and reliable, have been carefully tested, and failure will not result if directions are *closely* and *accurately* followed," she writes. "The 'dishes' made from them will be found suited to Southern tastes, Southern cooks and Southern markets, most of the articles called for being kept in every well supplied pantry. Other things can be procured from any first-class grocery store." The use of canned foods, for instance, represented a transformation of cooking during Emma's lifetime. When Emma called for canned crab, she was referring to new food

---

[38] Ferris, *The Edible South*, 86.
[39] Ibid., 90–91.

technology. Far from polemical, Emma's introduction focused on practicality.[40]

The politics of the so-called servant problem in the late nineteenth century were more evident in Emma's writings for the *Columbus Enquirer-Sun*. On the surface, she wrote in anticipation of the upcoming Thanksgiving and Christmas holidays, and tailored three articles of recipes—some new and some previously published in *Some Good Things to Eat*—for the upcoming celebrations. Yet she also chastised women for being unable to meet the demands of cooking and the kitchen. "What sensible man would presume to take charge of a business direct and manage his employees without first mastering the business down to the smallest details," Emma asked. "Yet we women, and we call ourselves sensible, too, marry and take upon ourselves the duties of a home, in utter ignorance, the majority of us, of the most important feature of the home—cooking and the kitchen." Emma argued, following in the tradition of domestic manuals, that the health and prosperity of the household depended on good food and the economic sense of the housewife. For this reason, she applauded that Columbus public schools taught cooking. At least part of her motivation for writing was to improve kitchen management. She feared that ignorance empowered cooks, mostly poor and African American women, at the expense of the middle- and upper-

---

[40] "Some Good Things to Eat," *The Eufaula* (AL) *Daily Times*, July 3, 1898; Jessamyn Neuhaus, *Manly Meals and Mom's Home Cooking: Cookbooks and Gender in Modern America* (Baltimore, MD: Johns Hopkins University Press, 2003), 17; N. D. Jarvis, "Curing and Canning of Fishery Products: A History," *Marine Fisheries Review* 50/4 (1988): 184 [180–85].

class white ladies. "It is no wonder that we are at the mercy of our cooks," she warned. "They soon discover our inability, and use, yes, and abuse us, too, at their pleasure."[41]

The cookbook was not a financial success. Few, if any, advertisements appeared in Southern literary magazines or newspapers. It may have drummed up business, though, for Emma's cooking classes, which catered to middle- and upper-class white women in Columbus. One cooking class numbered about seventy-five students in Columbus in the spring of 1900. "Delightful refreshments, all made by Mrs. Lane, were served, and the ladies were delighted with them," the *Columbus Daily Enquirer* reported. "The refreshments included sandwiches, wafers, deviled ham and a beautiful lot of bread. The wafers were chocolate, ginger, lemon, fruit and plain. At the conclusion of the afternoon's exhibition each lady was presented with a souvenir yeast cake."[42] Emma's teaching, combined with frequent moves of her family and selling off real estate and interests in family real estate, raises the question of the stability of the family's finances. She even expanded her advertising back to her hometown. "Wanted—To do fancy cooking of all kinds," one ad in the *Americus Times-Recorder* announced. "Special attention given to receptions." The love of food, the household politics of the late nineteenth century, and personal

---

[41] Emma Rylander Lane, "Cooking and the Kitchen," *Columbus* (GA) *Enquirer-Sun*, November 19, 1899.

[42] "Cooking Class Organized," *Columbus* (GA) *Daily Enquirer*, March 17, 1900.

economic uncertainty may all have influenced her public writings.[43]

After a flurry of cooking classes in southwest Georgia, the Lane family moved across the continent to Cananea, a copper mining town in Sonora, Mexico. It was an unusual move for a family that had never lived more than eighty-five miles from Americus. Davis, a telegraph operator for the Central of Georgia Railway in 1900, must have seen an opportunity with the Southern Pacific of Mexico Railroad and the wave of American investment in northern Mexico. The town expanded under William C. Greene, backed by powerful Wall Street investors, who formed the Cananea Consolidated Copper Company in 1899. The *Times-Recorder* reported Dave Lane, the youngest child in the household, worked as "an engineer of a stationary engine" in 1907 making $90 per month at age twelve. In many ways, though, the American enclave at Cananea resembled cities north of the border. Race and class divided the town. Mexican miners lived on discriminatory wages while Americans lived in relative affluence on the "Mesa" above them.[44]

------

[43] *Americus* (GA) *Times-Recorder*, January 20, 27, 1901.

[44] "Lane Funeral Will Be Held Tomorrow," *Arizona Daily Star* (Tucson), July 18, 1932; C. L. Sonnichsen, "Colonel William C. Greene and the Strike at Cananea, Sonora, 1906," *Journal of the Southwest*, 13/4 (Winter 1971): 343–68; John Mason Hart, *Empire and Revolution: The Americans in Mexico Since the Civil War* (Los Angeles: University of California Press, 2002), 145–47; Kelly Lytle Hernandez, *City of Inmates: Conquest, Rebellion and the Rise of Human Caging in Los Angeles, 1771–1965* (Chapel Hill: University of North Carolina Press, 2017), 104–106; "Comes to Old Home Alone

Far off in Cananea, Emma Lane died of pneumonia in 1904. "Relatives in Americus received yesterday morning the sorrowful tidings of the death of Mrs. Emma Rylander Lane," the *Times-Recorder* reported, "which occurred on Sunday at her far away home in Cananea, Mexico." The announcement of her death praised her "highest Christian virtues" and reminded readers of her father in the Civil War, but it made no mention of her cooking record.[45]

There were initial doubts that the family was going to be able to bring the body home from Mexico for burial. And yet, about ten days after her death, three of her four children brought the body back on a train, met additional relatives in Montgomery, and together finished the journey to Americus. "A large concourse of sorrowing friends met the body at the depot and attended the last sad rites," the *Times-Recorder* reported. "There was a profusion of very beautiful flowers, typifying the pure life and character of the one sleeping in the casket they adorned." Ministers from Calvary Episcopal Church and Furlow Lawn Baptist Church officiated the funeral services at Oak Grove Cemetery.[46]

The move to Mexico and the death of Emma fractured the Lane household. Thomas Lane, the eldest child, never seems to have left for Mexico in the first place. Annie Lane returned to

---

from Mexico: To Americus from Sonora Mex. Young Lad Came Alone," *Americus* (GA) *Times-Recorder*, August 15, 1907.

[45] "Death of Mrs. Davis T. Lane, Former Americus Lady Died Sunday in Mexico," *Americus* (GA) *Times-Recorder*, April 26, 29, 1904.

[46] "Funeral of Mrs. Davis Lane, Large Attendance of Friends at the Obsequies," *Americus* (GA) *Times-Recorder*, May 6, 1904.

Americus to marry Fred Markett less than a year before her mother's death. The youngest child, Dave, may have left Mexico for good when he took the train back alone in 1907. Three years later, at age fifteen, he resided with his sister and brother-in-law.[47] Carrie Lane may have stayed in Mexico longer than her siblings. The *Times-Recorder* reported in 1907 that she was visiting Americus from "Mexico City." She returned permanently by the end of the decade to marry Joseph Law.[48]

Davis stayed in Mexico. He and at least some of his children were present in 1906 when miners faced down what they saw as symbols of American capitalism and imperialism in northern Mexico. The strike and its backlash—what became known as the Cananea Massacre—killed dozens of miners and stoked criticism of the Mexican government that helped lead the country to revolution in 1910.[49] Between the strike and the revolution, the rest of Emma's children left Mexico. Yet Davis stayed until at least 1910. He married Carmen Gonzales and gained a stepson, Raul, in the marriage. The couple had two

---

[47] "Married at Cavlary Church: Nuptials of Miss Annie Lane and Mr. Fred Markett," *Americus* (GA) *Times-Recorder*, June 19, 1903; "People Who Come and Leave Town," *Americus* (GA) *Times-Recorder*, May 31, June 7, 1907; 1910 US Census, Militia District 748, Coffee County, GA, dwelling 24, family 27, pg. 2A, Frederick Markett, Dave Lane; digital image, Ancestry.com, accessed June 1, 2021; citing NARA microfilm publication T624, roll 181.

[48] 1910 US Census, Militia District 1635, Jenkins County, GA, dwelling 254, family 256, pg. 10B, Joseph Law, Carrie Law; digital image, Ancestry.com, accessed June 1, 2021; citing NARA microfilm publication T624, roll 199.

[49] Hart, *Empire and Revolution*, 148.

additional children, Jose and Santiago. The family relocated to Arizona during the Mexican Revolution and eventually anglicized the names of the two youngest children to Joseph and James.[50]

Demand for the Lane cake eclipsed the culinary artist and her cookbook in the early twentieth century. The popularity grew without public fanfare because the liquor involved necessitated reticence. Baking a Lane cake offered an excuse for having an open bottle of whiskey or brandy lying around the kitchen. After Alabama and Georgia enacted prohibition at the state level in 1907, more than a decade before the Eighteenth Amendment, the less said about the kitchen liquor the better. Even during Prohibition, Georgia newspapers occasionally mentioned the dessert between 1900 and 1930. In 1910, at a Georgia Weekly Press Association meeting, the Americus and Sumter County Hospital Association catered a meal that served broiled chicken, hot rolls, asparagus on toast, and a variety of sides. For dessert, diners selected from vanilla ice cream in cantaloupes, pound cake, and Lane cake.[51] In 1915, the *Miller County Liberal* reported that the "As You Like It Club" in Colquitt, Georgia, served its members quail on toast, dainty biscuits, coffee, as well as pound cake and Lane cake with

---

[50] 1920 US Census, Naco, Cochise, AZ, Enumeration District 0017, dwelling 97, family 101, pg. 4B, Davie T. Lane, Carmen B. Lane, Jose Lane, Santiago Lane, Raul Gonzales; digital image, Ancestry.com, accessed June 1, 2021; citing NARA microfilm publication T625, roll 46; "Lane Funeral Will Be Held Tomorrow," *Arizona Daily Star* (Tucson), July 18, 1932.

[51] "Finishing Plans to Entertain Editors," *Americus* (GA) *Times-Recorder*, June 30, 1910.

marshmallow charlotte, perhaps as a substitute for the boozy frosting.

The popularity of the Lane cake—despite or, perhaps, because of Prohibition—far exceeded the dessert's appearance in popular media. In 1930, Susan Myrick, associate editor of the *Macon Telegraph*, was stumped by a request for the recipe and asked readers to send in recipes. "I must declare my delight over the results," she remarked. "Twenty-six women were good enough to spend a two-cent stamp and a good deal of time and write me how to make the Lane Cake, and no less than a dozen women have stopped me on the streets, while a dozen more have phoned me about how to make the popular cake."[52] The first recipe, submitted by Emma C. Parker, came from Americus and from a copy of *Some Good Things to Eat* along with an explanation that Emma Rylander Lane came from one of the city's oldest families. Other women offered recipes with substitutes for the whiskey or brandy. Myrick's inquiry, along with the response, indicates that general knowledge of Emma's contribution to Southern cooking far outweighed her public acknowledgement.

Place, Memory, and Ghosts

While the connection between Emma Rylander Lane, Americus, and the Lane cake weakened in the twentieth century, the name "Rylander" remains part of multiple local landmarks. During the Great Depression, Jimmy Carter and his

---

[52] Susan Myrick, "Cooking Department: Number of Readers Submit Recipes for Lane Cake in Response to Inquiry," *Macon* (GA) *Telegraph*, January 26, 1930.

childhood friend, Alonzo Davis, traveled from Archery to Americus to watch movies in the Rylander Theatre.[53] The Rylander Ford Dealership, built in 1920, became, in the late-twentieth century, the international headquarters for Habitat for Humanity. Both buildings, named after Emma's brother, came long after her death.

The Lane cake, too, has been a local staple. When I mentioned this project to my barber, Kellette Heys Wade Sr., he offered to let me look through his mother's cookbooks. I was not disappointed. Martha Wood (1924–2019) had not one but multiple Lane cake recipes on scraps of paper and clippings from newspapers. In the same collection, the *Junior Welfare League...Cookbook* (1952) contained a recipe very similar to the original recipe.[54] Jimmy Carter, in *Christmas in Plains: Memories*, remembers Lane cakes as part of Depression-era holiday treats. It was his father who would make them. "I guess it would be more accurate to say that Mama never liked to cook, and welcomed my father into the kitchen whenever he was willing," Carter recalled. "He was always the one who prepared battercakes or waffles for breakfast, and he would even make a couple of Lane cakes for Christmas. Since this cake recipe required a strong dose of bourbon, it was just for the adult

---

[53] Jimmy Carter, *An Hour before Daylight: Memories of a Rural Boyhood* (New York: Simon and Schuster, 2001), 14, 95–96.

[54] *Junior Welfare League...Cookbook* (privately printed, 1952), 67; Martha Lorena Heys scrapbooks, undated, in possession of Kellette Heys Wade Sr., Americus, GA.

relatives, doctors, nurses, and other friends who would be invited to our house for eggnog."[55]

Other connections to Rylander landmarks, including places Emma would have known, are less obvious. In the early fall of 1973, Rosalynn Carter led Jacqueline Cook, a writer with the *Atlanta Journal and Constitution Magazine*, through the "haunted house" of Plains. The house, a circa-1850 Greek Revival plantation house built for Matthew Edmund Rylander, had already frightened generations when Jimmy and Rosalynn Carter rented it from 1956 to 1961. "I don't know when I first heard it was haunted," Rosalynn Carter told Cook. "Over the years, there were many bizarre occurrences, but one story I remember was that a light in the attic window was a candle kept burning by a lady so soldiers would know where to hide during the Civil War."[56] The house that Emma Rylander knew as her paternal grandfather's home lived on in local memory, but it created a general sense of unease.

[**Figures 8,9**] Black and white residents told Cook about a woman in a white dress who walked from Lebanon Cemetery toward the building. Other residents saw ghost animals or a light emanating from the spring across the road. Whispering voices and loud bangs came from one bedroom in particular.[57] By the 1930s, the children of Plains and Archery accepted the

---

[55] Jimmy Carter, *Christmas in Plains: Memories* (New York: Simon & Schuster, 2001), 50.

[56] Jacqueline Cook, "Haunted House at Plains," *Atlanta Journal and Constitution Magazine*, October 7, 1973.

[57] Ibid.

haunted house as fact. "The graveyard was bad enough," Jimmy Carter wrote in *An Hour before Daylight*, "but the haunted house was much worse. There were frequent reports of a woman who could be seen through the attic windows, wearing a long white flowing dress and carrying a candle, apparently looking for someone or something she had lost."[58] Carter recalled that he and his childhood friends bypassed the building by walking down the railroad instead of the highway.[59] Rosalynn Smith, too, in traveling to visit Ruth Carter, avoided the house by walking through the woods on the north side of highway.[60] The haunted footprint of the Rylander property played an oversized role in both Jimmy and Rosalynn Carter's memories of childhood.

The building is a simple plantation house with elements of Greek Revival architecture and a worrisome twist. There are two hidden rooms located between the first-story closets and the floor of an attic. Jack Carter, playing in the attic in the 1950s, discovered loose bricks in one of the two upstairs fireplaces. Removing the bricks enabled him to pull out the floorboards. This revealed a cavity—about the size and depth of a grave—containing a ladder and a chair. According to Cook, a second hidden room was discovered in 1973. This second room contained a Carter family treasure: a photograph of Jimmy and Rosalynn Carter on their wedding day in 1946 that

---

[58] Carter, *An Hour before Daylight*, 47. See also Jimmy Carter, *A Full Life: Reflections at Ninety* (New York: Simon and Schuster, 2015), 75–76.

[59] Carter, *Hour before Daylight*, 47.

[60] Cook, "Haunted House at Plains."

had slipped through the floorboards in the attic. The once-lost photograph had been trapped in the house for twelve years after the Carters moved to their present home on Woodland Drive.[61]

The unease that local residents have felt at the Rylander house has manifested itself in ghost stories that range from the intriguing to the absurd. Tales about slavery and the Civil War predominate, but so do stories about the stigmas associated with mental illness. Many of the traumas—and tragedies seemed to haunt the Rylander family in the nineteenth and early twentieth century—have morphed into a general discomfort with the property.

As a newcomer to Plains in 2015, I heard these stories, too. Patrick Rios, an intern with the National Park Service, took me to explore the abandoned house less than a week after my arrival. I went back again and again, sometimes alone, sometimes with Patrick, and sometimes in large groups on Saturday nights after a hearty Southern potluck and several drinks. My earliest research in the area, with Patrick's assistance, involved trying to understand what this house meant to the local community. Why was *this* house haunted? And did it have something to do with the Rylander family's unlucky streak in the nineteenth century? Emma's father's ambiguous Civil War death? Her own mysterious death in Mexico? Or any one of the many traumas connected to this place and this family?

Historians have a more unified opinion on the significance of foodways than they have about ghost stories and "dark"

---

[61] Ibid.; Rosalynn Carter, *First Lady from Plains* (New York: Fawcett Gold Medal, 1984), 38–39.

tourism. If studying the past through foodways has now been normalized, reliving the past through the supernatural is still suspect. Sarah Handley-Cousins, Tiya Miles, and many others who study places of trauma worry that ghost hunters exploit historical subjects for "cheap thrills."[62] Alena Pirok, in contrast, argues that ghost stories create their own layer of historical significance. "The relationship between ghosts and history is much older than contemporary tours," she reminds us, "and in most cases, these old tales lack the spooky or violent quality that characterize today's hauntings."[63] Ghost stories matter in Pirok's view because they contributed to the development of a preservation ethic in the early twentieth century.

Both perspectives are valid. Ghost stories can cheapen historical trauma and play into damaging stereotypes in the present. They are also, like food, a way that cultural values are transmitted within a community and to outsiders, like me, who show up for dinner. As for the Rylander house, its reputation

---

[62] Sarah Handley-Cousins, "Ghosts Are Scary, Disabled People Are Not: The Troubling Rise of the Haunted Asylum," *Nursing Clio*, October 29, 2015, https://nursingclio.org/2015/10/29/ghosts-are-scary-disabled-people-are-not-the-troubling-rise-of-the-haunted-asylum/; Tiya Miles, *Tales from the Haunted South: Dark Tourism and Memories of Slavery from the Civil War Era* (Chapel Hill: University of North Carolina Press, 2015).

[63] Alena Pirok, "Spirit of the Season," *History@Work*, October 24, 2016, https://ncph.org/history-at-work/spirit-of-the-season/; Pirok, *The Spirit of Colonial Williamsburg: Ghosts and Interpreting the Recreated Past* (Amherst: University of Massachusetts Press, 2022); Pirok, "Goodwin's Ghosts: Colonial Williamsburg's Uncanny Legacy," *The Public Historian* 41/2 (August 2019): 9–30.

as haunted seemed to overshadow everything else, including the fact that a future president and his family lived there. The ghost stories of the Rylander house first set me on this journey to understand the connection between this house, its extended family, and the region. That project came into closer focus when Michele Dunn, my friend and accomplished Southern cook, first asked whether there was any connection between Emma Rylander Lane and the haunted Rylander house. It helped narrow the questions I set out to answer in finding the last-known original copy of this book.

The local connections also confirmed how I wanted to use this cookbook as a public history product and ongoing project. The Friends of Jimmy Carter National Historical Park, a non-profit organization that owns the Rylander house, collaborates with the SAM Shortline Railroad for a regular murder mystery series aboard the train. The story line, written by Kim Fuller, always incorporates food. Raymond "Lee" Kinnamon, a retired history teacher and the mayor of Americus, plays the role of Benefield Martin, an aristocratic ne'er-do-well hoping to get his hands on some secret recipe. All royalties from the republication of *Some Good Things to Eat* are to be split between the Friends of Jimmy Carter National Historical Park, an organization on which I have had the pleasure of serving with Jimmy and Rosalynn Carter since 2017, and the Sumter Historic Trust.

A Note on the Editorial Method

The following is the original text of Emma Rylander Lane's *Some Good Things to Eat*, published in 1898 by the J. W. Burke Company of Macon, Georgia. The only known copy of the original book is in the Patrick Cather Collection of Auburn

University. This transcription recreates that text as closely as possible without encumbering the text with heavy notes and correcting simple typographical errors and inconsistencies. I have also added punctuation at times and standardized inconsistent capitalization (Icing to icing, for example) and spelling (such as mayonaise to mayonnaise, pine apple to pineapple, cocoanut to coconut, chrystalized to crystalized, yelk to yolk, mould to mold, geletine to gelatin, and so on). Other inconsistencies, such as tablespoon and tablespoonful, have been retained.

A word of caution: I am not a professional—and perhaps not even a competent—cook. I have not attempted to make these recipes, which were written for an era without temperature dials or modern refrigeration. Even where there is a standard conversion (moderate oven = 350–375°F; moderately hot = 375–400°F; hot oven = 400–450°F), it may take some time to familiarize oneself with this cookbook's instructions. My purpose in recovering, editing, and introducing this text is, first and foremost, to recover a fuller story of Emma Rylander Lane and preserve her work. While the following recipes are not necessarily easy, I hope that the republication of *Some Good Things to Eat* will make them accessible once again.

Some Good Things to Eat

Price, 50 cts.

Mrs. Emma Rylander Lane

Clayton, Alabama

My Best Cakes, Salads, Croquettes, Etc.

With A Few Choice Miscellaneous Recipes Kindly

Contributed By My Friends.

Mrs. Emma Rylander Lane,

Clayton, Ala.

Macon, Ga. Press of the J. W. Burke Company.

1898

To my mother, whose early training developed

in me a love for the culinary art, and

to my husband, whose discriminating

and appreciative appetite has been

my inspiration for nearly sev-

enteen years, I dedicate

this book.

Preface

The object of this book is to meet some of the most imperative needs of Southern housekeepers, and its price (fifty cents) places it within easy reach. The first thought of every woman when she assumes the duties of a home should be her kitchen, as the health, happiness and prosperity of a family depend largely upon the character of the food eaten and upon the wisdom and economy of the housewife. All of you love sunshine and sugar, and if you value your husband's sweet temper you *must* give him his three daily meals well cooked and properly served.

Only a limited number of recipes are here given, but all are known to be good and reliable, have been carefully tested, and failure will not result if directions are *closely* and *accurately* followed. The "dishes" made from them will be found suited to Southern tastes, Southern cooks and Southern markets, most of the articles called for being kept in every well supplied pantry. Other things can be procured from any first-class grocery store.

Should some of the directions seem tedious and too long, remember that expert cooks can overlook them entirely, while to the inexperienced full and explicit instructions are a necessity.

I beg to return most heart-felt thanks to those of my friends who have so kindly contributed to this book, and should it meet with their wants and with those of the public generally, it will be followed by a second volume embracing more of the needs of the kitchen and dining room.

Bread

Biscuits

Pastry

Wafers

Bread and Yeast.

The most important part of bread-making is to have good, reliable yeast. No matter how carefully the finest recipes are followed, good bread cannot be made from poor yeast. Neither can good results be expected from inferior flour, and great care in following directions is much more important than any amount of "nursing." Always remember that bread is much oftener ruined during the rising process, by too much, than by too little heat, and more often left to rise too much than not enough. When not risen enough, it is tight, close and hard, but never sour. When risen too much, it has the appearance of a coarse sponge, is dark in color, sour to the taste, heavy, indigestible and unfit for anything, unless it be for the pigs.

Good, Reliable Yeast Cakes.

Yeast cakes should always be made in clear, dry weather, never during a damp and rainy spell. Peel two large Irish potatoes, put them into a stew pan, with a handful of hops or peach tree leaves, green or dry, the hops or leaves tied in a cloth. Pour over them three pints of water and let them boil with the vessel covered until the potatoes are done. Take out the potatoes, mash them well with a fork, mix with them one pint of sifted flour, then pour to this the boiling water in which the hops and potatoes were covered. Beat with a spoon until perfectly smooth, adding one tablespoonful of salt, one of pulverized ginger and half a cup of sugar. While this mixture is lukewarm add to it one cup full of good liquid yeast, or two fresh yeast cakes, which first must be dissolved in one quarter cup of warm water.

If the weather is hot, let this stand one day in a cool place, and, if cold weather it must stand two days in a warm place. Beat it down frequently during the rising process, then add sufficient corn meal to make a stiff dough, and mold into cakes about half an inch thick. Dry these in the shade and as rapidly as possible, turning them several times during the day to keep them from souring. When they are nearly dry, break into small pieces, and when thoroughly dry crumble and put away in tied paper bags.

SUMMER LIGHT BREAD.

After dinner and not later than three o'clock, put into a small bowl half a yeast cake, or one tablespoon crumbled yeast, with half a cup tepid (not warm) water. When it dissolves add sufficient flour to make a batter so stiff that it will drop from the spoon like a thick jelly. Cover close[64] and let it stand in a warm (not hot) place about five hours. Add to this one cup tepid water; use enough flour to make another very stiff batter; cover again and let it remain until morning. (It should be mixed in a stone or granite vessel, large enough for the sponge to double itself in rising and not run over.) After breakfast, or about seven o'clock, add to the sponge one quarter cup of sugar, one heaping tablespoon salt, one scant tablespoon lard, one tea cup tepid water, and stir all together until the sugar and salt are melted. Sift two quarts flour into a tray, pour the liquid into it, mix into a stiff dough, using more flour if necessary, work or

---

[64] Lane used the word "close" in a peculiar way. It appears to mean "securely" here; elsewhere, as in "close tin box," it seems to just mean close-d.

45

beat until the dough is soft, smooth, very elastic and full of small blisters, remembering that this working or beating is *absolutely necessary* to make good bread. After it is beaten as directed, put it into a greased bowl or pan, grease the top of the bread with melted lard, cover with a cloth and put where it will keep warm but not get hot. When it has risen to double what it was when it was put in, turn it into the tray without using any more flour, work it a few minutes, mold into long loaves or rolls, (never put it solid in a round pan) put into pans well-greased on sides and bottom, grease top of bread and put to rise a second time, again covering with a cloth. When it doubles itself once more it is ready for the stove. Have the stove moderately hot when the bread is put in, keep a steady fire, turn the pans around once or twice during the baking, so that the bread will brown evenly. It should bake in forty or fifty minutes, according to the thickness of the loaves. When you take it from the stove, turn it out on a cloth, break one loaf or roll apart from the rest, press the broken part lightly with the fingers, and if found dry and elastic the bread is done; if it is the least sticky or close put [it] back in the pan as it came out, put it back in the stove and bake a few minutes longer. After it is done and out of the stove, glaze the top with melted butter. To properly cool it, spread on a table (not a pine one) a clean dry cloth, stand the loaves with one end on the cloth, the other resting on an inverted tin, and let them so remain until *quite* cold. Bread will keep fresh and moist many days, winter or summer, if put away in well-covered stone jars or close[d] tin boxes.

WINTER LIGHT BREAD.

Follow the directions given for bread in summer, using the same proportions except in place of half a yeast cake use a whole one, or two tablespoons crumbled yeast; have all the water warm, but not hot, melt lard before putting it in, and warm all the flour that is used. Never let the yeast or the bread get chilled, and *do not heat* it. Have each vessel warmed before using, keep yeast and bread out of draught while rising, and well covered with a thin piece of blanket or a thick well warmed cloth.

BEATEN BISCUIT.

For Lunches or Picnics

1 quart unsifted flour, 1 scant cup lard, 1 even cup cold water, 1 heaping teaspoonful salt.

Sift flour and rub lard well into it. Dissolve salt in the water and mix with flour and lard into a stiff dough. Beat until a little soft, work in a bit more flour, beat again, work in flour again, and continue this until the dough blisters and is very soft, smooth and pliable. Roll about half an inch thick, cut into round shapes about the size of a silver dollar, stick with a sharp fork and bake thirty or forty minutes in moderately hot oven. If baked too rapidly, they will be hard and tough. When done, glaze the top of each biscuit with melted butter, using for the purpose a cloth or soft brush. These are better after getting cold, and will keep fresh and nice many days, if put away in a close[d] tin box.

BEATEN BISCUIT.

For Tea, Or with After Dinner Coffee

1 quart unsifted flour, ½ cup lard, ½ cup fresh sweet butter, 1 cup fresh sweet milk, 1 *rounded teaspoon salt.*

Sift flour and salt together. Cream lard and butter together, rub it well into the flour, and mix with the milk into a stiff dough. Work and beat as directed in Beaten Biscuit for lunches, cut in the same shape and size, stick the same way, bake a little more quickly. Do not glaze the top, and serve hot.

VERY LIGHT BREAKFAST BISCUIT.

1 quart unsifted flour, ½ cup lard, 1 heaping teaspoon baking powder, 1 heaping teaspoon salt, ½ teaspoon soda, 1 cup *fresh buttermilk.*

Sift flour, salt, soda and baking powder together twice, rub lard into it, pour in buttermilk and mix with a large spoon, to a smooth soft dough. Roll to 1 inch thickness, cut and bake in moderately hot oven.

CRISP DINNER BISCUIT.

Use the same proportions as for Breakfast Biscuit, except take 1 ½ quarts flour, instead of only 1 quart, which will make a very stiff, firm dough. Work or beat until the dough begins to blister, and is quite soft and pliable. Roll to ½ an inch thickness, cut, stick each biscuit with a sharp fork, and bake (not too fast), a rich brown.

LUNCH BISCUIT.

Take a piece of well risen light-bread dough, roll to ½ inch thickness, cut into small round shapes, not larger than a silver half dollar, put them fully an inch apart, into well greased biscuit pans, let them rise just a little, and bake a delicate brown. They will be nearly all crust, and most delicious.
Aunt Odie.

CHEESE BISCUIT.

1 pint sifted flour, 1 teaspoon baking powder, 1 tablespoon lard, 1 tablespoon butter, 1 cup grated cheese, 1 teaspoon salt, cayenne pepper to taste, a little sweet milk.

Cream together the butter, lard, cheese and salt, sift together twice [the] flour and baking powder. Rub into the flour with a spoon the creamed mixture, put in a few dashes of cayenne pepper, and mix to a soft dough with sweet milk. Roll out the dough until very thin, cut into tiny biscuits and bake to a delicate brown.

Mrs. Odie Rylander Serrine, Greenville, S.C.

PLAIN CRISP PASTRY.

1 quart unsifted flour, 1 teaspoon baking powder, 1 teaspoon salt (heaping), 1 cup cold, stiff lard, 1 cup cold water (iced if possible).

Sift flour and baking powder together, rub lard into it with the back of a tablespoon, dissolve salt in water, and mix all to a stiff dough, still using the spoon, and working in more flour if needed. Do not put the hands into the dough or try to smooth it. Take from the mass about as much as is wanted for one rolling, and roll to the required thickness, handling only as much as is necessary. Put the pastry in the stove as soon as possible after mixing, and no matter for what purpose it is used, it should be baked slowly, and the top glazed with unbeaten egg white, before cooking.

VERY LIGHT DELICATE PASTRY.

1 heaping quart flour, sifted, ½ cup butter, ½ cup lard, 1 light teaspoon baking powder, 1 heaping teaspoon salt, 1 egg white, ¾ *cup ice water.*

Sift flour and baking powder twice together, put butter and lard on ice to harden, then cut both into the flour. Dissolve salt into the water, stir it with the egg white, then mix *all* to a very stiff dough, using a spoon for the mixing. Handle as little as possible, and if not to be used as soon as mixed put on ice, or it will ruin. This pastry must be slowly and carefully baked, as it is easily burned.

CHEESE WAFERS.

4 ounces sifted flour, 2 ounces butter, 2 ounces grated cheese, ¼ teaspoon salt, cayenne pepper to taste, 1 egg yolk.

Cream the butter, add beaten egg yolk, put in salt and pepper, rub in flour and cheese alternately, leaving a little flour for the last. Work with the hands until quite smooth, roll to ¼ of an inch thickness, cut into very small round wafers, and bake a delicate brown. These are very nice and suitable for teas, lunches or with after dinner coffee.
Mrs. Ed Parish, Clayton, Ala.

SWEET WAFERS.

2 eggs, 5 level tablespoons sugar, 6 rounded tablespoons sifted flour, 3 tablespoons melted butter, 1 teaspoon cold water.

Beat eggs and sugar smooth and light, add flour, then the melted butter and the cold water, this will make the batter stiff enough to drop, not pour. Have wafer irons moderately hot, perfectly clean and greased for the first wafer only, with lard or tallow. Drop the batter in with a teaspoon, having it about full, cook to a pale brown, move the wafer from the irons to a plate, using a knife, as that will easily slip under it. Roll while they are quite hot.

PLAIN WAFERS.

2 ¼ cups sifted flour, 1 cup fresh buttermilk, 1/3 teaspoon soda, ½ teaspoon salt, 1 teaspoon baking powder, 1 tablespoon melted butter, ½ tablespoon melted lard.

Sift flour, soda and baking powder together, add salt and buttermilk, beat until smooth, and last put in melted butter and lard, mix well, and bake in very hot ungreased wafer irons, using a heaping teaspoon of batter for a wafer.

ZEPHYR WAFERS.

Excellent.

½ tea cup sweet milk, 4 light tablespoons sifted flour, ¼ teaspoon salt.

Put flour in a small deep pan or bowl, pour over it half the milk, put in salt and beat until free from lumps, and quite smooth, add remaining milk, which should make a very thin batter. Have wafer irons quite clean, well greased for first wafer only, and not too hot, as these wafers are easily scorched. Put in a teaspoon level full for a wafer, and cook to a delicate brown.

Loaf

Cakes

General Directions for Cake Making.

In order to be a successful cake maker, there are several things necessary to carefully keep in mind. First and not the least important, is the best materials, namely, white, light dry flour—"Jaques & Tinsley's Best,"—if possible to obtain it; best granulated sugar, fresh eggs, reliable baking powder and rich, sweet butter.

In measuring or weighing cake materials be *perfectly accurate*, remembering that over or under weight, scant or heaping measure, unless so directed, will nearly always bring failure. When rich cakes are made, and egg yolks are used, beat them *well and just as soon as they are broken*, then they can be put aside until they are ready for use, without injury to the most delicate cake, beating them up a little, just as they are used.

Egg whites should not be whipped until *quite* ready for use, and *must* be put into the batter *immediately* after they are beaten and the whip removed. Allowing them to stand for even one minute will make the cake coarse grained, and a little tough.

On no account put the hands into the butter for creaming or into the batter for mixing or beating, some good cake makers to the contrary. The heat from the hands melts the butter and renders the batter oily and heavy, when every effort should be made to have it frothy and light. No one can expect to do first class work of any description without the necessary implements. In cake-making use a wooden bowl and a silver or wooden spoon for creaming butter and mixing batter; deep earthenware bowls for breaking eggs into and for beating the eggs, both whites and yolks, spoon-shaped gauze wire whips.

The first move toward cake-making is to clear the table of every article except such as are needed in the preparation of the cake. Next, prepare the baking pans, that is, clean and paper them ready to receive the batter as soon as it is mixed. Put out the requisite amount of material and *no more*. Sift the flour and baking powder together *just as many times* as directed, for the lightness and delicacy of many cakes depend largely upon that. More explicit directions for mixing will be found with the recipes, also directions for baking. [On] these few points carefully observe: Put the cake into the oven immediately after the batter is mixed and poured into the pan, first regulating the heat to suit the size and kind of cake to be baked, never forgetting that many more cakes are ruined by too little than too much heat, and be sure the stove is not so hot that it will have to be cooled off after the cake is put in.

Another point to be noted, do not use layer or muffin-tin recipes for loaf cake, for the reason that in most cases layer and muffin-tin batter is not firm and thick enough to make a good loaf, while, on the other hand, loaf recipes are not light and porous enough for best layers and muffin-tins.

Cake Making in Winter.

Warm flour and sugar before measuring or weighing, and keep warm until used. If milk or water is used, slightly warm that. Cream butter through warm (not hot) water, carefully rubbing every lump soft before the water is drained off or any sugar is put in, then beat and mix the cake as usual.

Cake Making in Summer.

For the beating and mixing get away from the heat of the kitchen, if possible, for a cool atmosphere helps to make a light cake. First thing unless the eggs have been on ice, put them in a large bucket *full* of cold water and let them stand at least half an hour before breaking. Cream the butter through cold water, then beat and mix in the ordinary way.

Cake Baking.

All layer cakes should be baked rapidly; all loaf cakes moderately fast or slow, according to thickness and kind of cake. To tell when all cakes are done, first they should leave the sides of the pan and wrinkle around the edges. When they reach that point press them with the tips of the fingers, very gently and near the middle of the cake. If done, the cake will be spongy and elastic, with only a slight finger print left. If not done, the finger prints will be deep and decided. All cakes, unless otherwise stated, are better if left to cool in the pans.

BROWN FRUIT CAKE.

(My Favorite Recipe)

1 dozen eggs, 1 pound flour, ½ pound flour extra for flouring fruit, 1 pound sifted sugar, 1 pound butter, 2 ½ pounds seeded and clipped raisins, 2 pounds washed and picked currants, 1 pound sliced citron, 2 pounds shelled almonds, ½ pint brandy or whiskey, ½ pint imported wine, 2 tablespoons cinnamon pulverized, 1 tablespoon allspice pulverized, 1 tablespoon mace

pulverized, 1 scant teaspoon cloves pulverized, 1 nutmeg grated.

The first step in making fruit cake is to prepare the fruit, then the pans, all of which should be finished the day before the cake is to be mixed and baked. To prepare the fruit, scald raisins in plenty of boiling water, drain and wipe perfectly dry with a towel, seed, clip and rub them well with flour, then sift out all the flour that does not stick. After currants have been well washed, picked and dried, flour and sift them the same way. Scald; peel and dry the almonds, then split each one in half. Thoroughly mix raisins, currants and almonds, then put them aside. Slice citron very thin, but do not flour it nor mix it with the other fruits. Prepare the pans by first greasing them with lard, next line the sides of each with three layers of brown paper, cutting it into small sections so it will fit smoothly without creasing. Grease each layer lightly to keep it in place. Put four layers in the bottom of the pan, greasing only the top piece. Mix the batter, as directed in "Old Fashioned Rich Pound Cake," add to it all the spices, beating them well into the batter. Next put in wine and brandy, mix thoroughly, and, last, lightly stir in the mixed fruits. Build the cake by first putting in the pans a layer of batter, then a sprinkling of citron (being careful not to let any of the citron touch the sides of the pan) and continue this until all the batter and citron are used, letting the top layer be batter. Bake carefully and slowly in a moderately hot oven, keeping the fire at an even, steady heat. It will require from two to four hours baking, according to the thickness of the cake. When nearly done it will leave the sides of the pan, and when quite done you can press lightly with the tips of the fingers and leave no impression. Let the cakes remain in pans until perfectly cold, ice *all over* and put away in close[d] tin boxes with three or four sound apples in each box. This will keep the cakes fresh and moist many months, and they improve with age, only be careful to look often into the boxes to see that the apples do not decay, and as they begin to speck replace them with sound ones. Under no condition should a fruit cake be cut before it is a month old.

BLACK FRUIT CAKE.

(Prize Recipe.)

1 dozen eggs, 1 pound sifted flour, 1 pound sifted sugar, 1 pound butter, 2 pounds seeded and clipped raisins, 1 pound cleaned currants, 1 pound finely sliced citron, 2 pounds un-shelled almonds, 1 cup syrup, ½ cup whiskey or brandy, 2 tablespoons allspice pulverized, 2 tablespoons cinnamon pulverized, 1 tablespoon cloves, 1 teaspoon soda.

Follow the directions given for Brown Fruit Cake, substituting for the imported wine the cup of syrup, after beating into it the teaspoon of soda.

OLD FASHION RICH POUND CAKE.

1 pound sifted flour, 1 pound sugar (granulated), 1 pound butter, 1 dozen eggs, ½ pint of brandy or alcohol, 1 large lemon, 1 teaspoon (rounding) baking powder.

Sift flour and baking powder together three times. Cream butter with half the sugar. Separate eggs, beat yolks very light, add to them remaining sugar, beat very light again, and mix well with creamed butter, add flour and well whipped whites, alternately, little at a time, beginning with flour. Last, put in brandy and juice of lemon. Pour into a deep ungreased pan, with two layers of white or brown paper in the bottom. Bake

58

slowly in moderately hot oven. When nearly done, it will leave the sides of the pan, when you can lightly press in the middle with the tips of your fingers and leave no prints, it is ready to take from the stove. Let it remain in the pan until cool.

PLAIN POUND CAKE.

1 pound sifted flour, 1 pound sugar (granulated), ¾ pound butter, 1 dozen eggs, 2 teaspoons (rounded) baking powder, 1 lemon (juice only).

Mix and bake the same as Rich Pound Cake, having the stove a little hotter and baking more rapidly.

DELICATE POUND CAKE.

1 pound sifted flour, 1 pound sifted sugar, ½ pound butter, 7 eggs, ½ pint sweet milk, 1 tablespoon baking powder.

Cream sugar and butter, add alternately milk and flour, which has been sifted three times, with baking powder. Last, beat in eggs, one at a time, giving several minutes beating to each egg. In baking follow directions in "Dainty Pound Cake."

DAINTY POUND CAKE.

1 pound sifted sugar, 1 pound sifted flour, ½ pound butter, ½ dozen eggs, 1 ¼ cup sweet milk, 2 heaping teaspoons baking powder.

Sift flour and baking powder together three times. Cream butter with half the sugar. Separate eggs, beat yellow light, add to them the remaining sugar, beat until light again, then mix well with creamed butter. Add flour and milk alternately, beginning and ending with flour, and, last, well beaten whites. As soon as smoothly mixed, pour into a deep ungreased pan lined on the bottom with heavy brown or white paper, and put at once into a moderately hot stove, and bake quickly but carefully, as it will easily burn if the fire is too hot, and will fail if baked too slow. To tell when it is done test the same as for Rich Pound Cake.

WHITE POUND CAKE.

1 pound sifted sugar, 1 pound sifted flour, ½ pound butter, 10 eggs (whites), 1 teaspoon (rounded) baking powder, 1 wineglass of alcohol.

Sift the flour and baking powder together four times; cream butter and sugar, add to it alternately flour and alcohol. Last, beat in well whipped whites, and pour at once into ungreased tins, using two layers of white paper in the bottom. Put into a moderately hot oven, slowly increasing the heat, being careful not to get it too hot. To tell when it is done test as directed for Rich Pound Cake.

GOLDEN POUND CAKE.[65]

1 pound flour, 1 pound sifted sugar, ½ pound butter, 16 egg yolks, 1 tablespoon baking powder, 1 cup brandy or whiskey, 1 cup sweet milk.

Sift the flour and sugar three times together. Cream butter with half the sugar. Beat the eggs with an egg whip until very light and foamy, add to them the remaining sugar, then beat again with a large silver spoon. When very light pour in the

---

[65] Lane's directions in this recipe are especially confusing. Sifting the flour and the sugar together seems to directly contradict later instructions.

brandy, stirring rapidly, and add it to the creamed butter. Beat in the flour and milk alternately, ending with flour. Prepare the pan and bake as in Rich Pound Cake.

BALANCE CAKE.

(The Best of All Plain Loaf Cakes.)

9 large eggs, the weight of 9 eggs in sugar, the weight of six eggs in butter, the weight of six eggs flour.

Sift the flour three times, cream well together, butter and flour. Beat yolks very light, add sugar, beat until light again, then mix with the creamed butter and flour. Last, beat in stiffly whipped whites and bake in a moderately hot oven.

WHITE CAKE.

(Large Size.)

12 egg whites, 3 cups sifted sugar, 6 cups sifted flour, 1 ½ cups butter, 1 ½ cups warm water, 3 *teaspoons baking powder.*

Sift flour and baking powder three times together. Cream the butter with half the sugar, and add to it alternately flour and warm water. Break the eggs into two bowls, six to each bowl. Whip one very light, add to it the remaining sugar, whip again, then add it to the batter. Last, whip the other six eggs stiff, beat them well into the batter, and pour into large ungreased tins with two layers of brown paper in the bottom. Bake slowly and carefully in a moderately hot oven.

WHITE CAKE.

(Medium Size.)

8 egg whites, 1 cup butter, 3 ½ cups sifted flour, 2 cups sifted sugar, ½ cup warm water, 1 *heaping teaspoon baking powder.*

Sift flour and baking powder together four times, cream butter with half the sugar, add alternately flour and warm water, whip whites until stiff, add to them the remaining sugar, whip again, beat them into the batter, and bake at once. Have two layers of brown paper in the bottom of the pan. Do not grease and do not bake too fast.

CUP CAKE.

(Large Size.)

4 cups sifted sugar, 6 cups sifted flour, 2 cups butter, 2 cups sweet milk, 12 eggs, 3 teaspoons baking powder.

Cream the butter with half the sugar, beat egg yolks with the remaining half, and mix all well. Sift flour and baking powder together four times, add to it the eggs and butter, little at a time, alternating with the milk, and, last, beat in well-whipped whites. Beat until smooth, and pour into a large ungreased tin with three layers of paper in the bottom. Bake slowly with a steady fire.

CUP CAKE.

(Medium Size.)

1 cup butter, 2 cups sifted sugar, 3 cups unsifted flour, 4 eggs, 1 cup sweet milk, 2 teaspoons baking powder.

Mix and bake as directed for Dainty Pound Cake.

LARGE LOAF SPONGE CAKE.

1 pound sifted flour, 1 pound sugar, 12 eggs, 2 heaping teaspoons baking powder.

Beat egg yolks perfectly light with an egg whip, add gradually the sugar, beating all the time, using a silver spoon this time; keep beating until the mixture is very light and foamy. Sift the flour and baking powder four times together. Whip the whites quite stiff, with a good pinch of salt, add them to the yolks, alternating with the flour, little at a time, saving a good portion of the flour to be used last. Beat only long enough to get the batter smooth and free from lumps. Bake at once in a hot oven. Put thick brown paper in the bottom of the pan, and do not grease paper or pan.

VERY BEST SPONGE CAKE.

6 eggs, 2 cups sifted sugar, 2 ¼ cups sifted flour, ½ cup cold water, 2 teaspoons baking powder.

Beat egg yolks very light with half of the sugar, dissolve the other half in the water, then mix. Beat whites stiff, mix again, and, last, beat in the flour which must be sifted four times, with the baking powder. Bake as directed in Quick Sponge Cake. This cake is better after standing twenty-four hours, if kept in a close[d] box, and if kept that way will be moist and good for a week.

QUICK SPONGE CAKE.

2 cups sifted flour, 2 cups sifted sugar, 10 eggs, 2 tablespoons cold water, 2 heaping teaspoons baking powder.

Beat the yolks very light, add sugar and beat until light again. Sift the flour and baking powder four times together.

Beat the whites stiff, adding a pinch of salt; add to yolks, alternating with the flour, a little each time, saving a good portion of the flour until the last. Beat until quite smooth, put in water and bake at once in a hot oven. Use ungreased tins with one layer of paper in the bottom.

ANGEL'S FOOD CAKE.

9 large or 10 small perfectly fresh eggs, 1 ¼ cup sifted granulated sugar, 1 cup sifted flour, ½ teaspoon cream tartar.

Sift the flour four times, break the eggs on a large flat dish, add a pinch of salt, and begin to beat, using an egg whip. When they are about half beaten add cream tartar and continue beating until very stiff. Remove the whip and with a large silver spoon beat in the sugar, and, last, sift the flour all at one time. Fold it in gently and lightly, and *just as soon* as the batter is smooth and free from lumps, put it into a clean, bright, ungreased tin, using no paper. Bake in a moderate oven, thirty or forty minutes. When done, turn the pan upside down, with the edges resting on the back side of large spoons, unless pans with little feet are used. Keep in this position until cool, then remove from the pan by cutting around the sides with a sharp knife.

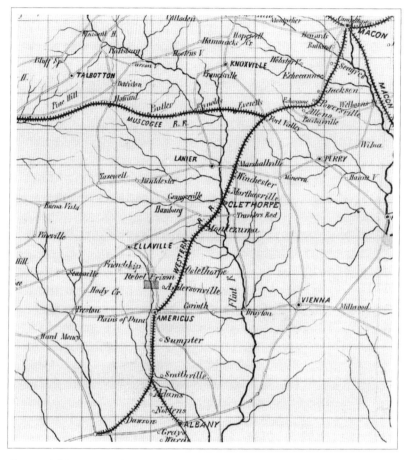

General Sherman's Campaign War Map, 1864.

Although Emma Rylander Lane published *Some Good Things to Eat* in Southeastern Alabama, she spent most of her life in Americus and Southwestern Georgia. Her maternal grandparents lived near Buena Vista and her paternal grandparents lived near the Plains of Dura (now Plains) and owned property in Macon.

	Dwelling-houses numbered in the order of visitation.	Families numbered in the order of visitation.	The name of every person whose usual place of abode on the first day of June, 1860, was in this family.	Age.	Sex.	White, black, or mulatto.	Profession, Occupation, or Trade each person, male and female, over 15 years of age.
	1	2	3	4	5	6	7
1	802	808	Jonathan Finch	45	m		Miller
2			Synthia "	51	f		
3			S. C. Williams	4	m		
4	803	809	William Gresham	24	m		Laborer
5			Mary "	35	f		
6			Charley "	23	f		
7			Wm. H. Parker	28	m		
8			Synthia M. "	14	f		
9			M. L. "	10	f		
10			M. J. "	5	f		
11			Mary P. "	1	f		
12	804	810	J. E. Rylander	24	m		Teacher
13	add	3	A. E. Rylander	24	f		
14		813	Emma "	4	f		
15			Carrie "	2	f		
16							

Post Office Americus

Dec 28 1860 Jany 31/61

U.S. Census, M653, roll 136, 1860, detail.

The Rylander family in 1860 consisted of Emory, Ann, Emma, and Carrie Rylander. Although coming from the planter class, Emory took the middle-class occupation of teacher after graduating from Emory College.

Courtesy National Archives and Records Administration

31	642	630	Murray Uintta	57	F	B	Cook	
32			— Virginia	12	F	Mu	At School	
33			— Henry	8	MB			
34	643	631	Rylander Ann E	34	F	W	Teaching	7
35			— Emma S	14	F	W	At School	
36			Carrie B	11	F	W	—	
37			Arthur A	9	MW		—	
38			Walter L	7	MW			
39			Mathis Evan P	20	MW		Farmer	1
40			Sue S	22	F	W	At Home	18

No. of dwellings,	7	No. of white females,	10	No. of males, foreign born,	
" " families,	7	" " colored males,	11	" " females, " "	
" " white males,	7	" " " females,	12	" " blind,	

U.S. Census, M593, roll 174, 1870, detail.

Ann Rylander raised four children as a widow of the Confederacy and taught school at the Furlow Masonic Female College. Emma, the eldest child, attended this school.

Courtesy National Archives and Records Administration

Furlow Public School postcard, ca. 1910.

The Furlow Masonic Female College, opened as a private school, became the site of the first public school in Americus, Georgia.

Courtesy Evan Kutzler

Emma Rylander and Davis Lane marriage license, 1881.

The middle years of Emma Rylander's life are the most difficult to
reconstruct. She lived with her mother in Americus until marrying
at age 25.

Courtesy Lake Blackshear Regional Library, Americus, Georgia

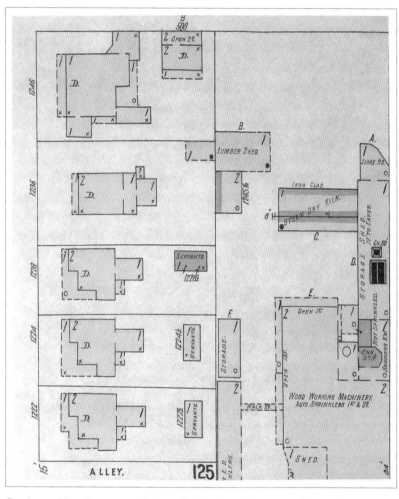

Sanborn Fire Insurance Map, Columbus, Georgia, Sheet 18, 1900.

Middle class households, including the Rylanders and the Lanes, relied on the labor, knowledge, and skills of African American women throughout the nineteenth and early twentieth century. Even when renting a house at 1224 5th Avenue, the Lane family employed an African American servant.

Courtesy Digital Library of Georgia

Parish house in Clayton, Alabama, 2022.

The Lane house in Clayton, Alabama, is not extant. Local tradition
states that Emma Lane baked the first Lane cake in the home of
Lucy Walker Parish.

Courtesy Evan Kutzler

Matthew Edmund Rylander house, 2015.

The Matthew Edmund Rylander house is called the Jimmy Carter Interim House by the Historic American Building Survey and the "haunted house" by locals. Built in the 1850s for Emma Rylander Lane's grandfather, this house is perhaps the only extant house where she spent considerable time.

Courtesy Patrick Rios

Entry hall of the Matthew Rylander house.

Children of the Great Depression knew the Rylander house as the "haunted house" and knew of the Lane cake as a holiday dessert. Lost was the connection between the family of the haunted house and the history of the cake.

Courtesy Library of Congress Historic American Building Survey

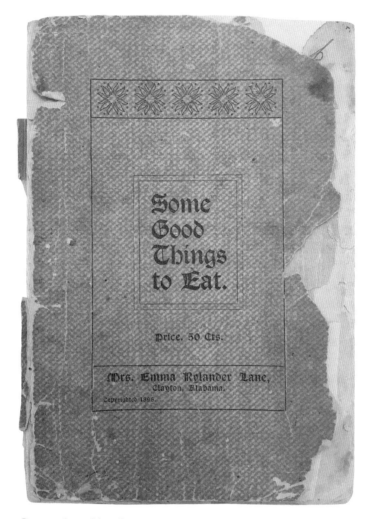

Original cookbook cover.

There are few extant copies of *Some Good Things to Eat*. WorldCat, a catalog representing 405 million book entries, identifies only one in participating libraries around the globe. Located in the Patrick Cather Collection of Southern menus and cookbooks, this rare book is preserved in a non-circulating section of the Auburn University library.

Courtesy Auburn University Libraries

Lunch

and

Layer

Cakes

VANILLA CREAM CAKES.

6 eggs, 2 cups sifted sugar, 3 ½ cups sifted flour, ½ cup boiling water, 1 scant tablespoon baking powder, [pinch of salt, and ¼ tablespoon vanilla].

Sift the flour and baking powder four times together, beat the egg yolks light, add sugar, half a cup at a time, and continue beating until the mixture is very light and creamy. Add the well whipped whites and a pinch of salt, mix well and add boiling water, stirring rapidly. Last, sift in all the flour, at the same time carefully folding or dipping it in until no dry flour is left, then beat rapidly until the batter is smooth and free from lumps. Put into small ungreased muffin-tins, and bake quickly. When cool, cut each one across with a sharp knife, take out a small part of each middle, fill the space with the following vanilla cream, put back together and ice.

These cakes are the nicest of all sponge cakes, and are fine without the filling, iced with plain boiled icing, and served with fruits or ices.

Filling—3 egg yolks (ice with whites), 1 ¼ cups sweet milk, ½ cup sugar, 1 tablespoon butter, 1 tablespoon *corn starch.*

Into a double boiler put one cup of the milk and half of the sugar, add butter, and when it reaches the boiling point pour in the starch, which must first be wet with the remaining milk. Stir as you mix, and when it has cooked a minute or two, pour into it, still stirring, the egg yolks and rest of the sugar, which must first be beaten until light. When it is the consistency of soft jelly remove from the fire, let it cool, and add one-quarter of a teaspoon of vanilla.

MUFFIN TIN WHITE CAKES.

8 egg whites, 2 cups sifted sugar, 2 ½ cups sifted flour, ½ cup butter, ¾ cup warm water, 2 ½ *heaping teaspoons baking powder*.

Cream the butter with half the sugar, sift the flour and baking powder four times together, add it little at a time to the creamed butter, alternating with the warm water. Last, whip the whites stiff, add to them the remaining sugar, mix well, then beat into the cake. Bake quickly in ungreased muffin-tins or in paper lined biscuit pans, cool thoroughly, cut into tiny squares or diamonds, with a sharp knife, and ice.

CUP CAKES.

(For Lunch.)

3 cups sifted flour, 1 ½ cups sifted sugar, 1 ¼ cups sweet milk, ¾ cup butter, 4 large eggs, 2 *teaspoons baking powder*.

Cream the butter and sugar, add well beaten yolks, sift the flour and baking powder together three times add to it the first mixture, alternating with the milk. Last, beat in the well whipped whites and bake quickly in ungreased muffin-tins.

FEATHER CAKES.

4 eggs, 1 *large* cup sifted sugar, 2 large cups sifted flour, ½ large cup butter, ¾ large cup of sweet milk, 1 heaping teaspoon baking powder, 1 small lemon (juice only).

Mix as directed in "Cup Cakes, for lunch," adding lemon juice last thing, and bake in muffin-tins.

CREAM SPONGE CAKES.

6 eggs, 3 ½ cups sifted flour, 2 cups sifted sugar, 1 cup sweet milk, 1 tablespoon baking powder.

Beat the egg yolks very light, add sugar, little at a time, and keep beating until very light again. Whip the whites well and add to the yolks and sugar, then beat in the cream, which must first be whipped until stiff. Last, sift the flour and baking powder together three times, sift into the batter all at one time, carefully fold (not stir) it in, slowly at first, then beat rapidly until the batter is smooth and free from lumps. Bake in a moderately hot oven in ungreased muffin-tins.

CHOCOLATE CAKE.

(Black Layers with White Filling.)

2 cups sugar, 1 ½ cups sweet milk, ½ cup butter, 2 ¾ cups sifted flour, 1 cup grated chocolate, 2 teaspoons baking powder, 4 eggs.

Stir well together one of the eggs, one cup of the sugar, the chocolate and half cup of the milk. Boil until quite thick, stirring constantly. Take from the fire, beat until cold and put aside. Sift flour and baking powder together twice, cream the butter with the other cup of sugar, add the remaining eggs after separating and beating them well. Last, put in flour and the remaining milk, leaving a little flour to be put in last. Flavor with lemon, beat in cooked chocolate and bake in four layers. Make a plain boiled icing, flavored with lemon, and put between the layers. Ice on the outside or not, as wanted.

CHOCOLATE CAKE.
(White Layers with Chocolate Filling.)

2 cups sugar sifted, ½ cup butter, ¾ cup sweet milk, 2 ½ cups sifted flour, 2 teaspoons baking powder, 1 teaspoon vanilla, 8 *egg whites.*

Mix and bake in four layers, as directed in "Lane Cake."

Filling.—Beat one egg light with one cup of sugar, or half cup if sweet chocolate is used, add one cup grated chocolate, half cup sweet milk or creamed lump of butter the size of an egg, (or no butter if cream and not milk is used). Mix altogether, boil until quite thick like jelly, stirring all the time. Beat until cool, add one teaspoon vanilla, spread thick between layers, and ice with plain boiled white icing, flavored with vanilla.

CITRON CAKE.

8 egg whites, 2 cups sifted sugar, 3 ¼ cups of sifted flour, 1 cup sweet milk, 1 cup butter, 2 teaspoons baking powder.

Mix and bake as directed in "Lane Cake."

Filling and Icing.—Take three egg whites, three cups sugar, twelve tablespoons of boiling water, and make a "Plain Boiled Icing." When it is ready for use, take out five tablespoonfuls, mix with it half pound grated or finely chopped citron, juice of half a lemon and one tablespoonful good wine, spread thickly between layers, and ice with remaining icing.

MACAROON CAKE.

8 egg whites, 3 cups sifted flour, 2 cups sifted sugar, 1 cup butter (scant measure), 1 cup sweet milk, two teaspoons baking powder, ½ teaspoon lemon extract.

Mix and bake as directed for "Lane Cake."

Filling and Icing.—Make a "Plain Boiled Icing," using for same three egg whites, three cups sugar, and twelve tablespoons boiling water. When it is ready for use, take from it four tablespoonfuls, which thicken with six almond macaroons, finely pulverized and sifted through a coarse sifter. Flavor with the juice of half a lemon and two tablespoonfuls good wine. Spread thickly between layers and ice with the remaining icing, using to flavor it the other half of the lemon.

LEMON JELLY CAKE.

1 cup butter, 2 cups sifted sugar, 1 cup sweet milk, 3 cups sifted flour, 4 eggs, 2 teaspoons of baking powder.

Sift the flour and baking powder together three times, separate the eggs, beat the yolks until very light, with half the sugar, cream the butter with the other half, beat all well together, and to the mixture add alternately flour and sweet milk until both are used. Beat this batter until it is light and smooth; and, last, beat in the well whipped whites. Pour into four ungreased paper lined pans, and bake immediately in a hot oven.

Filling.—One whole egg with the yolks of two more, (saving whites for icing), beaten light; with one cup of sugar, add one tablespoon hot water, one teaspoon corn starch, the juice of two large lemons, two tablespoons butter, and boil until a thick jelly, stirring constantly. Spread between layers and ice.

PLAIN JELLY CAKE.

5 eggs, 1 cup butter, 2 cups sifted sugar, 3 ½ cups sifted flour, two teaspoons baking powder, 1 cup sweet milk, [and 1 tumbler of an acidic jelly].

Mix and bake in four layers, as directed in "Lemon Jelly Cake."

Filling.—One tumbler acid jelly[66], melted and well mixed with one heaping tablespoon butter.

COCONUT CREAM CAKE.

1 cup sweet milk, 2 cups sifted sugar, 3 ½ cups sifted flour, 1 cup coconut milk, 5 eggs, 2 teaspoons baking powder.

Cream the butter and sugar, mixing in a little of the coconut milk, add egg yolks, which must first be beaten very light with an egg whip. Sift the flour and baking powder together three times, add it alternately with the remaining coconut milk, and, last, the well whipped whites, beat until smooth and bake in four layers.

Filling.—Two egg yolks (use whites for icing), one and a half cups sweet milk, half cup sugar, one tablespoon corn starch, one tablespoon of butter, 1 small coconut grated.

Mix and cook as for "Vanilla Cream," adding grated coconut while the cream is warm. Spread between layers and ice.

BANANA CAKE.

8 egg whites, 2 cups sifted sugar, ½ cup butter, ¾ cups sweet milk, 2 ½ cups sifted flour, 2 teaspoons baking powder, 1 teaspoon vanilla.

Mix and bake the same as "Lane Cake."

Filling.—Four large well ripe bananas, baked in their skins, until quite soft, peel, and, while hot, mash well with

---

[66] By "acid jelly," Lane means a jelly from more acidic fruits such as cranberries or citrus fruits.

piece of butter the size of an egg, and four tablespoons sugar. When cold, add a little grated nutmeg and four tablespoons of good wine. Spread between layers and ice.

CHEESE CAKES.

Of all layer cakes, I consider cheese cakes the least trouble to make, with small chance of failure; the best to the taste, the least expensive, and most satisfactory all around.

The cheese can be made any time there is an accumulation of egg yolks, and will keep for weeks, be the weather hot or cold. It requires no special skill in making, only follow directions carefully: Beat the eggs enough, and be sure the cheese is well cooked, (with no raw-egg taste left), before taking from the stove. In making layers, "Lane Cake" is best, with any cheese, for filling, suitable to taste or materials at hand. If the cheese is ready made, the best and least expensive layer is the one used for "Lemon Jelly Cake."

LANE CAKE.

8 egg whites, 1 cup butter, 1 cup sweet milk, 2 cups sifted sugar, 3 ¼ cups sifted flour, 2 teaspoons baking powder, 1 tablespoon vanilla.

Sift the flour and baking powder together three times, cream the butter and sugar until perfectly light, add to it alternately, little at a time, milk and flour, until all are used, beginning and ending with flour. Last, beat in the well whipped whites and vanilla. Bake in four layers, using medium sized pie tins, with one layer of ungreased brown paper in the bottom of each tin.

Filling.—Beat well together eight egg yolks, one large cup of sugar, and half a cup of butter. Pour into a small, deep stew pan and cook on top of the stove until quite thick, stirring *all the time*, or it will be sure to burn. When done and while still hot, put in one cup of seeded and finely clipped raisins, one wine-glass of good whiskey or brandy and one teaspoon of vanilla. Spread thickly between the layers and ice. It is much better to be made a day or two before using. My prize cake, and named not from my own conceit, but through the courtesy of Mrs. Janie McDowell Pruett, of Eufaula, Ala.

ORANGE CHEESE CAKE.

(Use "Lane Cake" for Layers)

Filling.—8 or 10 egg yolks, 1 cup sugar, ¼ cup butter, 1 large orange, 1 small lemon.

Beat the eggs and sugar together, add butter, and cook in a double boiler, stirring often. When it begins to thicken, add the grated rind and juice of the orange and lemon, and cook until a thick jelly, still frequently stirring. When cool spread between the layers and ice.

LEMON CHEESE CAKE.

Use "Lane Cake" for layers, and make the same as "Orange Cheese Filling," except use no orange and three large lemons.

PINEAPPLE CHEESE CAKE.

8 egg whites, 2 cups sifted sugar, 3 ¼ cups of sifted flour, 1 cup butter, 1 cup sweet milk, 2 teaspoons baking powder.

Mix and bake as directed for "Lane Cake."

Filling.—Take one small-size can of grated pineapple, and strain through a coarse sieve, so as to get out *all* the juice, or as much as possible. Beat eight egg yolks with one cup sugar, add two tablespoons butter, put into a double boiler over a hot fire, and stir occasionally, until the butter is melted, then add the pineapple juice and cook until quite thick, still stirring frequently. Remove from the fire, and when perfectly cold put in what is left of the pineapple. Spread thickly between the layers and ice.

NUT CHEESE CAKE.

8 egg whites, 4 egg yolks, 1 cup butter, 2 cups sifted sugar, 3 ¼ cups sifted flour, 1 cup sweet milk, 2 teaspoons baking powder.

Cream together the butter and sugar, add the well-beaten yolks, sift the flour and baking powder together three times, add it alternating with the milk, and, last, beat in the well whipped whites. Bake in four layers.

Filling.—Take the four egg yolks left from the cake, and three more which will be left from the icing, beat them together with three-quarters of a cup of sugar, add to them one tablespoon of butter, and cook in a double boiler until thick. Make a boiled icing using the three egg whites left from the cheese. When it is ready for the cake, take a heaping tablespoon of it, and mix it with the cheese. Flavor with vanilla, add a tablespoon good whiskey, one cup chopped English walnuts; spread between the cakes and ice with the remaining icing.

Tea

and

Ginger

Cakes

and

Icing

Tea and Ginger Cakes.

Do not raise a family without making tea or ginger cakes for the children once a week. Otherwise, you rob childhood of one of its rights, also of one of its chief joys. These cakes are easily made, and if thoroughly cooked and put away in well covered stone jars, will keep fresh and moist for more than a week.

RICH TEA CAKES.

4 eggs, 1 ½ cups sugar, ¼ cup lard, ¾ cup of butter, 1 quart sifted flour, 2 teaspoons baking powder.

Cream the butter and lard with one-half the sugar, beat the eggs very light with the other half; mix all, and add to it the flour and baking powder, which must first be sifted twice together. Work into a smooth dough, using enough flour to keep it from sticking too much to the hands and board. Roll to half an inch thickness, cut into round shapes, put into biscuit pans and bake a delicate brown. When quite cold, put away in a well covered stone jar.

PLAIN TEA CAKES.

2 eggs, 2 cups sugar, 1 cup butter, ¾ cup fresh buttermilk, ½ teaspoon soda, 1 ½ quarts sifted flour.

Rub the butter well into the flour, beat the eggs and sugar until light, beat the soda into the buttermilk. Mix all well together, pour into the flour and butter and work until smooth, adding enough flour to make a very stiff dough. Roll thin, cut into any desired shape, put into biscuit pans and bake quickly.

YELLOW KID TEA CAKES.

½ cup butter, ½ cup lard, 2 cups sugar, ½ cup sweet milk, 2 quarts unsifted flour, 2 teaspoons baking powder, 10 egg yolks.

Beat the eggs very light, add sugar and beat until light again; cream the butter and lard together. Mix all, add milk and mix again. Sift flour and baking powder twice together, pour the mixture into it, and work into a smooth, firm (not stiff) dough, using more flour if needed. Roll to half an inch thick, cut into any desired shape, and put into biscuit pans and bake in moderately hot oven.

These cakes should be made of yolks left from making Small Loaf White Cake, and are the very best of all the tea cake family.

LEMON TEA CAKES.

1 cup butter, 2 cups sifted sugar, 2 whole eggs [and] yolks of two more, 1 lemon, 1 pint flour sifted.

Cream the butter and sugar, beat in the eggs, one at a time, add half the flour. Mix well, then put in the grated rind and juice of the lemon, work to a smooth dough with the remainder of the flour, using still more if necessary. Roll very thin, cut into any desired shape, put into biscuit pans and bake quickly.

LUXION TEA CAKES.

5 eggs, 4 cups sugar, ½ cup sweet milk, 2 quarts flour (sifted), 2 teaspoons baking powder, 1 ½ pounds butter, ½ pound washed and picked currants, ½ pound clipped and seeded raisins, ½ pound finely sliced citron, 1 ounce vanilla, 1 tablespoon cinnamon pulverized, 1 tablespoon allspice pulverized.

Sift twice together the baking powder and flour, rub into it one pound of the butter. Beat together until light the eggs and one cup of the sugar, add to them the milk and vanilla, pour this mixture into the flour and work into a smooth dough, using more flour if needed. Divide this dough into three equal parts and put aside. Take the remaining butter and sugar, cream together with the spices, divide this into two equal parts, and set aside. Mix the fruits and divide them into three equal parts. Take one part of the dough, roll like pie-crust into an oblong shape, spread with one part of the creamed butter, sprinkle with one part of the mixed fruits, roll into a long round roll, something the shape of a large sausage, press (not roll) with the rolling pin to one and a half inch thickness, cut with a sharp knife into small shapes, put into buttered biscuit pans and bake slowly. Use up the three divisions in the same way.

These cakes are excellent, and if put away after they are quite cold, in close[d] tin boxes, will keep moist and fresh several weeks.

GINGER CAKES.

2 or more quarts sifted flour, ½ cup lard, ½ cup butter, 1 cup sugar, 2 cups syrup, 5 eggs, 2 tablespoons ginger, 1 teaspoon soda.

Cream the butter and lard together, add to it the well beaten eggs and sugar, pour in syrup, next the ginger, and last, the soda dissolved in a little warm water. Mix all well and work in enough flour for a smooth dough, and stiff enough to roll easily without sticking. Cut into shape desired, put into biscuit pans, and bake carefully as they are easy to burn.

GINGER SNAPS.

1 or more quarts sifted flour, 1 cup syrup, 2/3 cup sugar, 1 cup lard, 1 tablespoon soda, 2 tablespoons pulverized ginger, ¼ teaspoon cayenne pepper.

Cream the lard and sugar together, beat the soda into the syrup, mix, add the ginger and pepper. Beat all well together and work into it enough flour for a very stiff, smooth dough. Roll very thin, cut into small round cakes, and put into biscuit pans and bake quickly. When cold, put into stone jars, cover well, and they will keep moist several weeks.

ICING.

When making icing, do not feel discouraged over any failure. The quality of the eggs and (whether fresh or stale) the character of the sugar, and the atmosphere, have quite as much to do with icing as the method of making it.

Sometimes icing will not stiffen, no matter how carefully it is made, and then again the same process will bring perfect results. After twenty years' experience and careful study I am never quite sure of success. For stiffening and rapid drying use cream tartar, acetic acid, tartaric acid or lemon juice, putting in very little at a time, as it is easy to get too much. When a large quantity is made and a crust forms on the top, before all is used, soften it with a few drops of boiling water beaten in. Two eggs and two cups of sugar made into Plain Boiled Icing will be sufficient to ice an ordinary sized cake.

PLAIN BOILED ICING.

White of 1 egg, 1 cup granulated sugar, 4 tablespoons boiling water.

Put the sugar into a perfectly clean, bright pan. Pour over it the boiling water, put it on a hot fire and stir carefully back and forth, (not round and round, as that will make the icing grain), until the sugar is all dissolved. Remove the spoon, wash it clean, dry it, and when the icing has boiled a few minutes dip up a spoonful, pour it back slowly, and if it runs from the spoon in a fine thread it is done. Take it from the stove and pour slowly on the well whipped egg white, beating carefully as you pour, and continue beating until it is cool. Flavor to taste, and if the icing runs, put in a pinch of tartaric acid. Double the quantity for a medium size cake.

CHOCOLATE ICING.

1 cup grated chocolate, ½ cup sweet milk, 1 cup sugar, or a half if chocolate is sweet, 1 egg, 1 teaspoon vanilla.

Beat the egg light with sugar, add the chocolate, stir until smooth, add the milk, and cook until thick and pasty, stirring constantly. When cool, add the vanilla. If for a large cake, double the quantity.

RAW ICING.

Use pulverized sugar for this, and sift it through a fine wire or very coarse muslin. Break the eggs, using the whites only, into a bowl, not more than three for one making; beat them only enough to slightly bubble, then add the sugar, one tablespoonful at a time, beating very hard after each time the sugar is put in. Continue this until the icing is of the desired consistency, and add a small bit of tartaric acid and flavor to taste.

Salads

and

Mayonnaise

Salads.

In making salads, no small amount of skill and care is necessary, if you desire them to be dainty and appetizing. The fruits and vegetables required should be well selected, using only such as are sound, fresh and unbruised. The mixing should be done with a silver fork, lightly and gently, not stirring, but with more of a tossing of the materials together to prevent their being sloppy or mushy. Nothing used should be ground through a sausage mill, but cut with a sharp knife into small bits, or chopped using for the purpose a regular chopping knife, and a chopping bowl. On *no account* must the hands ever be put into the salads, unless you want them to be tight and gummy. They are much better if mixed several hours before needed, and put on ice.

Taste and circumstances should govern the style of serving, but nothing is prettier than to serve on fresh lettuce leaves. In the following recipes apples are largely used, but celery or headed lettuce can be substituted, according to preference or convenience.

CHICKEN SALAD WITH CELERY.

1 young chicken, 2 or more bunches celery, 1 firm, juicy apple, 2 hard boiled eggs, (yolks only), ½ cup vinegar, 1 teaspoon dry mustard, 2 teaspoons sugar, 1 tablespoon white mustard seed, 2 tablespoons melted butter, salt, black and red pepper to taste.

Prepare the chicken as for chicken salad, with apples, and after it is cooked and cut, measure it and use an equal quantity of celery cut into half inch pieces with a sharp knife. Mix lightly, using a silver fork, adding the water in which the chicken was boiled. Mash together the egg yolks, dry mustard and sugar, mix lightly again, pour over this the melted butter, sprinkle in the mustard seed, add vinegar, season to the taste with salt, red and black pepper. Mix thoroughly with as little stirring as possible.

CHICKEN SALAD, (WITH APPLES).

1 young chicken, 3 hard boiled eggs, 5 firm, juicy apples, ¼ tea cup vinegar, 1 tea cup mayonnaise.

Cut the chicken as for frying, put it into a stew pan with two scant teaspoons of salt, three cups of cold water, and let it cook slowly until very tender and the bones will slip, remove the bones, chop into moderately small pieces, mix with the water in which it was boiled, add the coarsely mashed eggs, then the apples, which must be peeled, and cut into small bits, then the vinegar, and, last, mayonnaise.

CELERY SALAD.

2 cups cut celery, 1 cup chopped apples, 2 scant teaspoons dry mustard, 4 scant teaspoons sugar, 1 scant teaspoon salt, 4 hard boiled eggs, ½ cup vinegar.

Cut the celery into half inch pieces, with a sharp knife, chop the apples into small bits, rub together the egg yolks, sugar and mustard. Mix all lightly, sprinkle with the salt a very little black and red pepper, mash the eggs with a fork, and add, last; stir in the vinegar, and just before serving cover the whole with half a pint of whipped cream, or it may be omitted, according to the taste.

IRISH POTATO SALAD.

2 cups mashed potato, ½ cup sweet cream, ¼ cup vinegar, 4 tablespoons melted butter, 3 hard boiled eggs, 1 teaspoon salt, 1 teaspoon dry mustard, 2 teaspoons sugar.

Beat or stir the cream into the potatoes, add to them the well-chopped eggs, melted butter, and mix well, rub the sugar, salt and mustard together, mix it with the vinegar. Pour all over the potatoes, mix well with a fork and serve cold after standing several hours. A small bit of finely cut raw onion, put in just before serving, is a great improvement to those who like the onion flavor.

BEEF SALAD.

1 ½ cups cold roast or boiled lean beef, 2 hard boiled eggs, 1 teaspoon dry mustard, 1 teaspoon celery seed, ½ teaspoon white mustard seed, 2 firm, juicy apples, 2 tablespoons melted butter, 2 teaspoons sugar, ½ cup vinegar, ½ cup mayonnaise, salt, black and cayenne pepper to taste.

Chop the beef into small pieces, mash the eggs with a fork, cut the apples into tiny bits with a sharp knife, and stir all together with a silver fork. Mix the sugar and mustard well, add that, next the butter and vinegar, then the seeds, salt and pepper, and, last, the mayonnaise. It is better to [let it] stand several hours before serving.

BRAIN SALAD, (FINE.)

1 set beef brains, 5 hard boiled eggs, 2 hard, juicy apples, ¼ cup vinegar, ½ cup mayonnaise, 4 tablespoons melted butter, 2 tablespoons tomato catsup, 1 teaspoon celery seed, 1 teaspoon white mustard seed.

Soak the brains several hours in salt water, pour this out and scald in boiling water, remove skin and boil a few minutes in clear water, drain and wipe gently with a dry cloth, cut (not mash) into small pieces, add the chopped apples and finely cut eggs, sprinkle in the seeds, pour in the melted butter, mayonnaise, catsup and vinegar. Mix all at one time, lightly and gently, using for the purpose a silver fork. Put in the salt, black and red pepper to taste. Lightly mix again and serve quite cold, first putting it on ice if possible.

The success of this salad depends upon the way it is mixed. If it is mashed at all or stirred much it will be soft, watery and a failure. It is fine if properly made.

SARDINE SALAD.

3 firm, juicy apples, 2 boxes French sardines, 2 lemons, 4 hard boiled eggs, 1 teaspoon dry mustard, ½ teaspoon salt, ½ cup vinegar, ½ cup mayonnaise, two tablespoons sugar, black and cayenne pepper to taste.

With a silver fork mash the sardines into small pieces, mixing well with the oil in which they were packed. Add to them the juice of the lemons, the eggs chopped fine and the apples peeled and cut into small pieces. Mix the sugar, salt and mustard together, add next the pepper and vinegar, and last the mayonnaise.

EMERGENCY SALAD.

Empty a can of chipped beef into a bowl, cover it well with boiling water, and let it stand until the water is cold. Drain off the water, dry the beef with a cloth, and clip it into small pieces with scissors, cover it with mayonnaise, and you have a very nice, easily made salad. Four hard boiled eggs chopped and a tablespoon each of celery and white mustard seed will improve it.

EGG SALAD.

6 hard boiled eggs, 2 tablespoons melted butter, 1 teaspoon celery seed, ½ teaspoon white mustard seed, ½ teaspoon salt, ¼ cup vinegar, ¼ cup mayonnaise, 1 apple.

Chop (not mash) the eggs into small bits, cut the apple into small pieces, mix lightly, sprinkle in the salt, celery and mustard seed, pour over the melted butter, vinegar and mayonnaise, with black and red pepper to taste.

TENDERLOIN SALAD.

2 pounds tenderloin (pork), 3 hard boiled eggs, 5 firm, juicy apples, 3 tablespoons melted butter, 1 tablespoon white mustard seed, ¼ cup vinegar, 1 cup mayonnaise.

Cut the tenderloin into pieces the size of a hickory nut, sprinkle lightly with salt, put into a stew pan with two and a half cups cold water, cover and stew gently, frequently turning the pieces about until it is very tender, and only a little water is left. Chop the meat moderately fine, mix it with the water in which it was cooked, add the eggs, which first must be mashed with a fork, next the chopped apple, and mix lightly. Sprinkle in the mustard seed, pour over the melted butter, vinegar and mayonnaise, with salt, black and red pepper to taste.

TONGUE SALAD.

1 fresh beef tongue, (medium size), 4 tablespoons melted butter, 4 hard boiled eggs, 1 small onion, 1 teaspoon celery seed,

1 teaspoon white mustard seed, 3 tablespoons tomato catsup, ¾ cup mayonnaise, 5 firm, juicy apples.

Wash the tongue well and soak all night in strong salt water. Put to boil with the onion in cold water, using a moderately large vessel and plenty of water; cover and boil gently until very tender. Peel while hot and remove all fat, gristle, etc. Chop (not grind) fine, add eggs, cut into small pieces, the apple peeled and cut into bits, sprinkle in the seed, add the melted butter, tomato catsup and mayonnaise, and mix well with a fork, adding salt, black and red pepper to taste.

CRAB SALAD.

1 small can of crabs, 4 hard boiled eggs, half teaspoon dry mustard, ½ teaspoon salt, 4 tablespoons melted butter, 1 lemon (juice only), 1 teaspoon celery seed, ¼ cup mayonnaise, ¼ cup vinegar, black and red pepper.

Empty the crabs into a large bowl and carefully remove the small bits of shell, mash the yolks of the eggs to a paste, with the salt and dry mustard. Chop the egg whites and add to the crabs, sprinkle in the celery seed, pour in the lemon juice, vinegar and mayonnaise, mix gently, put in red and black pepper, to taste, and serve cold.

CHEESE SALAD.

2 cups grated cheese, 4 hard boiled eggs, ½ tea cup salad dressing, salt, red and black pepper to taste.

Mash the eggs well with a fork, add salt and pepper to taste, mix well with salad dressing, fill a salad dish with alternate layers of the grated cheese and egg mixture, beginning and ending with cheese.

HAM SALAD.

Grind through a mill the waste bits of lean [meat] and fat of a boiled ham. Measure and use in equal portion of well mashed hard boiled eggs, season with black and red pepper and moisten with mayonnaise and a very little vinegar and melted butter, using more or less butter according to the quantity of fat in the ham.

SALMON SALAD.

1 can salmon (large size), 4 hard boiled eggs, 1 teaspoon dry mustard, 1 teaspoon salt, ¼ teaspoon black pepper, 1 teaspoon sugar, 4 tablespoons melted butter, 1 tablespoon white mustard seed, 1 tablespoon celery seed, 2 tablespoons tomato catsup, 3 tablespoons Worcestershire sauce, ½ cup vinegar.

Remove skins and bones from the salmon, chop the egg whites, rub the egg yolks, mustard, sugar, salt and pepper to a paste, then gently but thoroughly mix all the ingredients, using a fork for the mixing, and serve cold.

MAYONNAISE.

(For Bottling.)

11 egg yolks, 1 cup sugar, 1 cup butter, half cup sweet milk or cream, 1 tablespoon dry mustard, 1 scant tablespoon salt, 1 teaspoon black pepper, ¼ teaspoon cayenne pepper, 1 ½ pints vinegar.

Beat the eggs and sugar together, until very light, add the salt, pepper and mustard. Mix well, boil the milk and pour it over the mixture, stirring rapidly. Boil together the vinegar and butter, pour while steaming hot to the eggs, milk, etc., stirring rapidly again, until well mixed. When quite cold, strain through a wire sieve, bottle, cork and put in a cool place. This makes a quart and keeps nicely for months. It is best to make it when you make Citron or Macaroon Cake, as they each require eleven egg whites, leaving the yolks to be used in some way as wanted.

MAYONNAISE.

(For Immediate Use.)

3 eggs, 1 cup sweet milk or cream, 1 cup vinegar, 1 tablespoon sugar, 1 tablespoon dry mustard, 1 tablespoon salt, 1 scant tablespoon butter.

Separate the eggs and beat them until perfectly light, then mix and stir in the vinegar, then the cream. In another vessel rub together the sugar, salt and mustard, then thoroughly mix all, and last, add the butter. Boil until thick and creamy, stirring rapidly all the while.

PLAIN MAYONNAISE.

1 cup vinegar, 1 tablespoon dry mustard, 1 tablespoon sugar, 1 tablespoon butter, ½ teaspoon salt, ½ teaspoon black pepper, 2 eggs.

Rub together the sugar, mustard, salt and pepper, add to it the well beaten eggs. Boil the butter and vinegar together, and pour while hot over the eggs, etc., stirring rapidly until nearly cold.

SALAD DRESSING.

1 egg yolk, 1/8 teaspoon cayenne pepper, ½ pint olive oil, 1 tablespoon vinegar.

Beat the egg yolk with salt and pepper, then beat in the oil, [one] drop at a time, and last, beat in the vinegar, very little at a time. Do not mix in a warm atmosphere or it will not be stiff.

Rob. Crawford, Eufaula, Ala.

MIXED MUSTARD.

2 tablespoons dry mustard, 1 teaspoon sugar, ¼ teaspoon salt, 1/8 teaspoon black pepper, 1/8 teaspoon red pepper, 1 tablespoon grease from a boiled ham, yolk of one hard boiled egg, ¼ cup vinegar.

Mash the egg yolk smooth with the mustard, sugar, salt and pepper, add the ham grease (while hot), slowly stirring as you pour. Last, stir in the vinegar and mix to a smooth paste. Mrs. Ed. Parish, Clayton, Ala.

Croquettes

and

Dessert

Croquettes.[67]

In mixing croquettes, have the mass as soft as can be molded, and if convenient roll them on a block of ice before putting in the raw egg and cracker crumbs. When ice cannot be used, mix the mass, then allow it to get perfectly cold before molding. The vessel for frying them in should be several inches deep, more than half full of lard, (or whatever is used in place of it), and the lard be *steaming* hot. When the croquettes are done, drip them on a soft, thick cloth, or on blotting paper, before serving. Carefully follow these instructions, and your croquettes will be juicy, crisp and most delicious. More important than all, they will not be unwholesome, as these dainties usually are.

Liver Croquettes.

2 pounds calf's liver, 2 hard boiled eggs, 1 raw egg, 1 small onion, ½ cup cracker crumbs.

Peel the liver and chop it very fine, mash the eggs fine with a fork, mix and add bread crumbs, the onion (cut into small bits), raw egg, salt and black pepper to taste. Work well with the hands, mold, dip and fry as for all croquettes.

---

[67] Lane expected readers to have extra cracker crumbs to use in the rolling process of preparing croquettes.

BRAIN CROQUETTES.

1 set beef brains, 2 hard boiled eggs, 1 raw egg, 3 tablespoons melted butter, ¼ cup sweet cream or milk, ½ cup cracker crumbs.

Prepare the brains the usual way, that is, soaking in salt water, scalding and peeling. Mash them very fine with a fork, grate the boiled eggs, mix and add to it the cracker crumbs, melted butter and beaten raw egg. Season to taste with salt, black and red pepper. Mix well with the hands, mold, roll in cracker crumbs and raw egg, then in the cracker crumbs again and fry in hot lard. Serve hot.

SALMON CROQUETTES.

1 large sized can of salmon, 2 hard boiled eggs, 1 raw egg, 1 small onion, 3 tablespoons melted butter, ½ cup cracker crumbs or mashed Irish potatoes, ¼ teaspoon salt, black and red pepper.

Remove all the bones and skin from the salmon and mash fine with a fork, add potatoes or [cracker] crumbs, whichever is used, mix with the salmon, add the well-mashed boiled eggs, the onion (finely cut), the salt, red and black pepper to taste, and last, the raw egg lightly beaten. Work well with the hands, mold, roll, dip and fry in the usual manner for croquettes.

TONGUE CROQUETTES.

1 beef tongue, medium size, 2 hard boiled eggs, ½ cup cracker crumbs, 2 tablespoons melted butter, 1 raw egg, salt, black and red pepper to taste.

Put the tongue to boil in plenty of unsalted cold water, that is, cover it well with water, let it boil slowly, and when quite done, peel, remove all fat and gristle, and chop fine. Add to it one cup of the water in which it was boiled, melted butter, cracker crumbs, the well mashed boiled eggs, and salt, red and black pepper to taste. Last, stir in the raw egg, after beating it well, mold with the hands, roll in the cracker crumbs, then in the raw egg, cracker crumbs again, and fry in hot lard.

BEEF CROQUETTES.

1 ½ cups cold roast or boiled lean beef, ½ cup cracker crumbs, 1 cup fresh sweet milk, 2 hard boiled eggs, 1 raw egg, 2 tablespoons melted butter, salt, red and black pepper to taste.

Chop the beef very fine, add to it the well mashed boiled eggs, melted butter, and mix well. Put in the sweet milk, cracker crumbs, salt, pepper, and the raw egg well beaten. Mix, mold, roll in cracker crumbs, then in the raw egg, in cracker crumbs again, and fry in hot lard.

CHICKEN CROQUETTES.

1 young, fat chicken, 2 hard boiled egg yolks, 2 ½ cups cold water, 1 scant tablespoon salt, [raw egg, and cracker crumbs].

Dress and cut the chicken as for frying, without salting, put it into a stew pan with the salt and cold water, cover close and stew gently until *very* tender. Take from the fire, remove the bones and skin, and chop or grind fine, pour over it the water in which it was boiled, (about [a] cupful it should be), add the well-mashed egg yolks, salt, red and black pepper to taste. Work into a smooth mass with the hands, cool thoroughly, mold, dip in cracker crumbs, in the raw egg, in cracker crumbs again, and fry in hot lard. These are the richest and juiciest of all croquettes.

TENDERLOIN CROQUETTES.

2 pounds pork tenderloin, 3 boiled eggs (yolks only), ½ cup cracker crumbs, ¼ cup of sweet milk.

Cut the tenderloin into pieces about the size of a hickory nut, put into a stewpan with two cups of cold water and half a tablespoon salt, cover and cook slowly, occasionally turning the pieces about. The water should nearly all be absorbed by the time it is done, and tender. Take it from the fire, chop fine, add what water is left, the well-mashed egg yolks, cracker crumbs, sweet milk, and last, season with black and red pepper and more salt if needed. After working well with the hands, shape, roll and dip the usual way for croquettes, and fry a delicate brown.

FRUIT SALAD, (VERY FINE).

3 large oranges, 3 large well ripe bananas, 1 large juicy apple, 1 small coconut, ½ pound malaga grapes, ½ pound crystalized cherries, 1 small can grated pineapple, 1 cup good wine, 1 cup sugar.

Peel the oranges and clip into small bits with scissors, carefully getting out the seed, quarter the bananas, slice very thin, cut the apple into small pieces, grate the coconut, cut the grapes into halves with a sharp knife, and the same for the cherries. Mix all, add the sugar, pineapple and wine, and serve alone, as it needs nothing to make it better, except standing overnight in a cold place.

FRUIT SALAD AND CREAM.

1 large can white cherries, ¼ pound crystalized pineapple, 1 lemon, 4 mellow apples, 6 very ripe bananas, ¼ pound citron, ½ cup sugar, ½ cup sweet wine.

Drain the juice from the cherries and do not use it. Remove the stones and with scissors clip each cherry in two, chop the pineapple and citron until almost a paste, cut the bananas into quarters, then slice them thin, grate the apples, grate all the yellow rind of the lemon and squeeze out the juice, add the sugar and wine. Mix all at one time with a fork, and as lightly as possible to prevent getting watery. Serve very cold with whipped cream.

BISQUE CREAM.

1 pint sweet cream, 4 egg whites, 1 lemon, 3 tablespoons sweet milk, 6 almond macaroons, ¼ cup sifted sugar.

Roll the macaroons until fine, and sift through a coarse sieve, whip the cream and add sugar, then macaroons, then the wine and lemon juice, and last, the stiffly beaten egg whites. If not as sweet as wanted, put in more sugar. Serve very cold. Do not let it stand too long after being mixed.

MACAROON CREAM, (DELICIOUS).

1 cup sugar, ½ pint of boiling water, ½ pint white wine, 2 heaping tablespoons corn starch, whites of 6 eggs, ½ cup cold water, ½ dozen almond macaroons, 1 lemon.

Put the sugar, wine and boiling water together in a double boiler, and stir until the sugar is dissolved. Mix the corn starch with the cold water, putting in a small pinch of salt, add this to the sugar and wine, stirring rapidly. When it thickens like jelly, take it from the stove and stir in the egg whites, which must first be beaten until stiff. Return to the fire, cook a few minutes longer, still stirring. When a little cool, add the macaroons, which must first be finely pulverized, and last, the grated rind and juice of the lemon. If the macaroons are damp and sticky, heat them slightly, and when cold again they will be crisp and dry. This must be served quite cold, with whipped cream.

LEMON CREAM.

5 eggs, 2 large juicy lemons, 2 cups sugar.

Beat the egg yolks and sugar to a cream, add the grated rind and juice of the lemons and cook in a double boiler until thick and pasty, stirring constantly, pour into it the well whipped whites, still stirring; cook a minute longer and take from the fire. Serve cold in custard glasses.

PINEAPPLE CREAM.

1 cup sugar, 1 pint boiling water, juice from 1 small can pineapples, 2 heaping tablespoons corn starch, whites of 6 eggs, ½ cup cold water, pineapple after the juice is taken out.

Put the sugar, boiling water, and pineapple juice together, in a double boiler, and stir until the sugar is dissolved. Mix the corn starch with the cold water, putting in a small pinch of salt. Add this to the sugar and juice, stirring rapidly. When it thickens like jelly, take from the stove and stir in the egg whites, which must first be beaten until stiff. Return to the stove and cook a few minutes longer, still stirring. When a little cool add the remaining pineapple. This must be served quite cold, with whipped cream or boiled custard.

CHOCOLATE FLOAT.

1 quart sweet milk, 4 eggs, ½ cup sugar, 4 tablespoons grated chocolate.

Put the milk into a double boiler, beat together the sugar, egg yolks, and chocolate, and stir it into the milk as it comes to a boil. Cook a few minutes, still stirring, then pour slowly over the well beaten whites, and keep stirring until well mixed. While still hot, flavor with vanilla and add sugar to taste, depending on whether or not sweet chocolate is used. Serve cold in small glass cups.

BANANA FLOAT.

6 large bananas well ripened, 6 tablespoons of sugar, 1 lemon, whites of 2 eggs

Mash the bananas until smooth, add sugar and the juice of the lemon. Mix well, beat the eggs to a stiff froth, stir in lightly. Serve as soon as mixed, covering each dish with whipped cream.

SNOW PUDDING.

1 ½ cups sugar, 1 pint boiling water, 2 heaping teaspoons corn starch, 5 eggs, ½ cup cold water, 1 pint sweet milk, 1 cup grated coconut, ¼ teaspoon vanilla.

Put the boiling water and one cup of sugar in a double boiler, and stir until the sugar is dissolved. Mix the corn starch and cold water to a paste, adding a pinch of salt, add this to the sugar and water, stirring rapidly until it thickens like starch. Take from the stove, stir in the well-beaten whites of the eggs, return it to the stove, and cook a few minutes, still stirring. When not quite cold, mix well with the coconut, which must first be spread on a flat dish, and kept in the sun or under the stove several hours. Beat the egg yolks and remaining sugar until light, heat the milk to the boiling point, pour over the eggs, stirring repeatedly. Return to the stove a few minutes, still stirring. When cold, flavor with vanilla, put a little on top of each dish of snow and serve quite cold.

CREAM PUDDING.

2 [tea]spoons baking powder, 6 eggs, 2 cups sugar, 2 cups sifted flour, ½ cup cold water.

Beat the egg yolks very light with half the sugar, dissolve the [other] half in the cold water, and mix all. Beat the whites stiff, with a pinch of salt, add them [to the egg yolks and sugar], sift the flour and baking powder twice together, beat in slowly until the batter is smooth, and bake in four layers.

Sauce.—Put into a double boiler one pint of sweet milk, and when it comes to the boiling point add to it, beaten together, one whole egg and the yolks of two more, and eight tablespoons sugar. Stir till it begins to thicken, cool, flavor to taste and spread between the layers. Beat the other two whites, with two tablespoons sugar, spread over the top, put in the stove and brown.

Mrs. Ed. Parish, Clayton, Ala.

ALMOND PUDDING, (EXCELLENT).

10 eggs, 1 ½ cups sifted sugar, 1 cup cracker crumbs, 1 cup almond flour.

Shell, blanch, beat and sift one pound almonds to make the cup of flour. Beat the egg yolks light with the sugar and add to them the almond flour, beat the whites until stiff, putting in a pinch of salt, and add them, alternating with the cracker [crumbs]. Bake in a buttered pan or pudding dish, and serve with whipped cream flavored with vanilla.

Mrs. Mattie E. Bivins, Americus, Ga.

PEACH PUDDING.

Line a deep dish or a pan with plain crisp pastry. Stick holes in the bottom with a sharp pointed fork to keep it from puffing, and bake a delicate brown. Fill two-thirds full with canned peaches, well-sweetened, cover with a meringue made from six egg whites beaten stiff, with six scant tablespoons sugar and one tablespoon wine. Return to the stove, brown slightly, and serve hot with cream.

CHERRY PUDDING.

3 tablespoons corn starch (heaping), 5 eggs, 1 quart sweet milk, 2 cups sugar, 1 cup canned, preserved or crystalized cherries.

Put the milk into a double boiler, beat very light the egg yolks and one cup of the sugar, add to it the corn starch wet with about one-fourth of a cup of cold water. Mix well and pour to the milk as it comes to a boil, stirring rapidly. Add a pinch of salt and keep stirring until it is thick like soft jelly. Remove from the stove and pour into a buttered pan or pudding dish, bake in a moderately hot oven until it becomes firm, cover the top with the cherries, draining off the juice if canned cherries are used. Cover with a meringue made from the egg whites and remaining sugar. Flavor with vanilla, return to the stove and slightly brown.

SUMMER CHARLOTTE.

2 quarts fresh sweet milk, 8 eggs, 8 tablespoons sugar, 8 tablespoons corn starch, ½ pint cold water.

Put the milk on the stove in a double boiler. Beat the egg yolks very light with the sugar, add to them the corn starch wet, smooth with the cold water, also a good pinch of salt. Mix well and add to the milk as it comes to a boil, stirring rapidly, and continue boiling until quite thick, still stirring. Take from the fire, and when cool enough to handle, squeeze through a very thin bag, beat into it the well-whipped egg whites. Flavor with vanilla, pour into molds and put on ice or in a cool place. Serve quite cold, with whipped cream, sweetened and highly flavored with good wine.

CHERRIES IN THE SNOW.

1 cup sugar, ½ pint of boiling water, ½ pint white wine, 2 heaping tablespoons corn starch, whites of 6 eggs, ½ cup cold water, ½ pound of crystalized cherries and 1 lemon.

Put the sugar, wine and boiling water together in a double boiler and stir until the sugar is dissolved. Mix the corn starch with the cold water, putting in a small pinch of salt. Add this to the sugar and wine, stirring rapidly. When it thickens like jelly take it from the stove and stir in the egg whites, which must first be beaten until stiff. Return to the fire and cook a few minutes longer, still stirring. When a little cool, add the cherries, and last, the grated rind and juice of the lemon. This must be served quite cold with whipped cream or boiled custard.

Ices

and

Pickles

Lemon Sherbet.

8 large juicy lemons, 1 pound of sugar, ½ box gelatin, ½ gallon boiling water, ½ gallon cold water. Soak the gelatin in one pint of the cold water until well swollen and soft, add to it one pint of boiling water and stir until well melted. Take the other three pints of boiling water and pour on the sugar, stirring until that is dissolved. Grate the yellow rind from the lemons, squeeze out the juice, stir *everything* well together, then add the cold water, carefully take out the lemon seed and freeze.

Strawberry Ice Cream.

2 quarts of strawberries, 2 pints sugar, 6 egg whites. Mash the strawberries well, mix with the sugar and let them stand an hour, or longer will not hurt. Strain them through a bag, pressing out all the juice. Measure it and add an equal portion of unskimmed sweet fresh milk or sweet cream, but not until the juice is in the freezer[68] and thoroughly chilled, or the milk will curdle. When it begins to freeze put in the well-beaten egg whites, and freeze as usual.

---

[68] Ice box.

Nut Ice Cream.

Make a plain boiled custard, using the proportions of one egg, one cup sweet milk, and one heaping tablespoon sugar. Boil the milk with half the sugar, beat the eggs unseparated, with the remaining half, pour the boiling milk on the beaten eggs, stirring rapidly. Measure, and to each quart of custard add one cup of *finely* chopped nuts, but do not put in the nuts until the cream begins to freeze. Almonds, English walnuts, roasted peanuts, and Pistachio nuts are best. When Pistachio nuts are used, flavor the cream with vanilla and bitter almonds. For the almonds use vanilla flavoring only, and lemon for the walnuts and peanuts.

RICH ICE CREAM.

2 quarts of fresh sweet cream, 8 eggs, 2 cups sugar.

Put the cream to scald in a double boiler, beat the egg yolks very light, add the sugar, and beat until light again, add the well-whipped whites, and stir all together into the cream, just as it comes to a boil. Cook two or three minutes, still stirring, strain through a coarse sieve, cool, flavor to taste and freeze.

BISQUE ICE CREAM.

Make the cream by the above recipe, and just as it begins to freeze add one dozen almond macaroons, pulverized and sifted through a coarse sieve. The cream should be first flavored with vanilla or bitter almond. This is one of the finest of all frozen desserts.

ICE CREAM.
(No Eggs or Cooking, and Very Fine).

1 gallon sweet milk, *fresh* and unskimmed, 1 pound sugar, ½ box gelatin, 1 pint boiling water, 1 pint sweet rich cream.

Soak the gelatin in half a pint of the milk until quite soft, and in about half an hour pour on it the boiling water and stir until dissolved. While still warm add the sugar and stir until it is melted. Put in the remaining milk. Flavor to taste. Pour into the freezer, and when it begins to freeze add the cream.

CLARET ICE CREAM.

2 quarts fresh sweet cream, 1 quart fresh sweet milk, 1 pint claret wine, 3 cups sugar.

Scald the milk, add the sugar while it is still hot, stirring until it is all dissolved. When cool, add the cream, mix well, [put] into the freezer, and when it begins to thicken, pour in the claret, first having it iced to prevent the cream from curdling.

MAKING PICKLES.

Use only fresh, sound, unbruised fruits or vegetables, and do not wash them unless cleanliness demands. When washing is necessary, drip, then dry them thoroughly, wiping gently with a dry cloth. Use no vinegar except such as you believe to be *pure and strong*. Where at all convenient put the pickles into small jars, quarts being the best size. The recipes here given are few, but *very* choice, and perfectly reliable. Follow them closely and success is certain.

SWEET PICKLE.

This can be made of plums, figs, peaches, cherries, or almost any fruit. 4 pounds brown sugar, 1 quart vinegar, 8 pounds fruit, mace, allspice, cloves and cinnamon to taste.

Select sound, ripe fruit, wash and dry it before weighing. Make a syrup of the sugar, vinegar and spices, boil until it begins to thicken, then put in the fruit, but only so much as the syrup will well cover. Boil steadily eight or ten minutes, lift out the fruit with perforated dipper, put it on a flat dish and drain the syrup back into the kettle. Put in the remainder of the fruit in relays, only so much each time as the syrup will cover, until all has been boiled the same length of time, taken out, drained the same way, and put into jars. The syrup which has been thinned by the fruit juice must now be boiled until quite thick, nearly the consistency of honey, and poured hot over the fruit. This is a most delicious pickle and one that keeps well.

PEAR PICKLE (VERY BEST.)

10 pounds pears, after peeled and quartered, 4 ½ pounds sugar, ½ cup water, 1 quart strong vinegar, a few sticks cinnamon and a few whole cloves.

Make a syrup of the vinegar, water and sugar, and when it comes to a boil put in the pears and spices. Cook the pears until tender, then take them out and put to cool on flat dishes. After which, put into jars. Boil the syrup twenty minutes after the pears are out, then pour it boiling hot over them, and seal when quite cold.

Mrs. A. H. Alston, Clayton, Ala.

MIXED PICKLE.

1 gallon chopped cabbage, 1 ½ gallons chopped green tomatoes, 1 quart chopped onions, 1 pint chopped green peppers, without seed, 2 tablespoons salt, 2 tablespoons cinnamon, pulverized, 2 tablespoons allspice, pulverized, 2 tablespoons dry mustard, 2 tablespoons sugar, 4 ounces turmeric, 2 ounces celery seed.

Prepare the vegetables early in the morning, put them into a stone jar, sprinkling in the salt, and let it stand until the evening, and then put in a bag and drip all night. Next morning put them in a brass or porcelain kettle, add the sugar and mustard, cover well with good vinegar, and boil slowly, until quite tender. Just before taking from the fire add the spices, turmeric and celery seed. Put into jars and seal while hot.

This pickle is very fine, easily made, ready for use as soon as thoroughly cold, and, best of all, will keep indefinitely. Mrs. Geo. Peach, Clayton, Ala.

SWEET PEACH PICKLE.

Select ripe, perfectly sound press peaches, peel them, weigh and to each pound of fruit use half pound of brown or granulated sugar. Pack the peaches, with one whole clove sticking in each peach, in quart or half gallon jars, sprinkling sugar all through with a thick layer on top. Let them stand twenty-four hours, and the juice of the fruit and the sugar will make a thick syrup. Drain this off and add to it an equal quantity of good vinegar. Let it come to a boil, and when cool pour over the peaches. Repeat this boiling three mornings, pouring it over hot the last time, and seal it air tight. Follow directions carefully, and you

will have delicious pickles with no danger of their softening or fermenting.
Mrs. Rosa Few Zimmerman, Greer's, S.C.

CABBAGE PICKLE.

2 large white cabbages, cut fine, ½ dozen large onions, cut fine, 1 cup sugar, 1 ounce turmeric, 1 teaspoon cayenne pepper, 1 box mustard (small size).

Mix the cabbage and onions, rub the mustard, sugar, pepper and turmeric well together, mix all and cover with vinegar. Let it simmer two hours, and when cold it is ready for use. A fine, rich mustard pickle.
Mrs. Mattie E. Bivins, Americus, Ga.

BRANDY PEACHES.

Select sound, ripe, *unbruised* press peaches. Peel them, stick one whole clove into each peach, *pack* them carefully into quart or half gallon jars, filling to within one inch of the top. Now pour the jar half full of cold water, then drain it off, being careful not to pour out the peaches. Add to the water an equal portion of alcohol, sweeten to taste, (quite sweet is suited to the average taste) with loaf sugar, and be sure to stir the liquid until every particle of sugar is dissolved. Pour this over the peaches, filling the jars to the brim. Close air-tight and put away undisturbed for three or four months. These peaches are the very finest I have ever tasted, will keep indefinitely without softening, improve with age, and possess the rare quality of being pure, as alcohol is seldom if ever adulterated.

Wine

And

Cordial

BLACKBERRY CORDIAL.

3 quarts of berries, 1 quart of best whiskey or brandy, 1 table-spoon whole cloves, and sugar to taste.

Select large thoroughly ripe berries, pick them carefully, but do not wash them. Put them in a one gallon jar, sprinkle the cloves all through as you put them in, pour in the whiskey, cover close and let them stand two days, then press out all the juice, strain and put in sugar to taste, making it very sweet. Stir until the sugar is all dissolved, bottle and cork tight. Is ready for use as soon as made, keeps indefinitely, and is invaluable for teething babes.[69]

Mrs. A. V. Lee, Clayton, Ala.

VERY FINE GRAPE OR BERRY WINE.

This wine can be made of blackberries, strawberries, huckle-berries, cherries, or from any variety of grape or scuppernong.

The fruit must be well dried, if washed, but is better if carefully picked and not wet. Mash the fruit well, and to every gallon measured after it is mashed add one quart of boiling water. Let it stand twenty-four or thirty-six hours, as most convenient, then press and strain through a cloth. To every gallon of juice add two and a half pounds of granulated sugar, if for a slightly acid wine, and if for sweet, three pounds. Stir until the sugar is thoroughly dissolved, pour into jugs, three quarts only to a gallon jug, cork loosely, with just enough pressure to the corks to keep them from falling out. Put in a dark place, and do not disturb until settled cool weather, as by that time all

---

[69] Please don't give this to babies.

fermentation is finished. Pour off carefully, so as not to get any dregs from the bottom, strain through a thick cloth; bottle; and to each quart put about one dozen large clipped but not seeded raisins. Cork tightly, put into a dark closet for several months, and it is ready for use, although it is better after longer keeping. This wine, if made exactly by directions, is the finest domestic wine I have ever tasted, and after several years ripening, is almost equal to the best imported.

PEAR WINE.

Use perfectly ripe pears. Grate, press and strain. To every gallon of juice add two and a half pounds granulated sugar. Stir until the sugar is all dissolved, pour into wide-mouthed stone jars, and cover with a cloth. Every morning, for six or seven [days], remove what scum rises to the top, and stir well each morning. At the end of that time strain through a cloth, put into jugs, and for several weeks cork loosely, then tightly. These directions, if carefully followed, will insure you excellent wine. Mrs. J. A. Foster, Clayton, Ala.

APPLE WINE.

To every gallon of fresh sweet cider put two and a half pounds granulated sugar. Stir until the sugar dissolves, pour into stone jars, cover with a coarse cloth tied over the top, then put away in a dark place until quite cool weather, so that all fermentation will be over. Strain through a cloth; bottle and cork tightly, and set away for several months, when it will be ready for use, and very fine.

Tea

Chocolate

And

Miscellaneous

Tea, (Hot and Iced).

To every cup of tea wanted use one teaspoon of tea leaves and one cup of boiling water. Always make it in [an] earthen pot, which should be half filled with boiling water and allowed to stand until the pot is well heated. Pour out this water, put in the quantity of tea leaves required, cover them well with freshly boiled water, let it steep (on no account boil) three or four minutes, then pour in the remaining boiling water, and serve *at once.*

In making tea to be iced use the same proportions, and follow the same directions, except drain the tea from the leaves after it has stood not longer than five minutes.

CREAM CHOCOLATE, (THE VERY BEST).

1 egg, ½ cup sugar, 5 tablespoons grated chocolate, 2 ½ cups unskimmed sweet milk, 2 ½ cups boiling water, ¼ teaspoon vanilla.

Pour the boiling water on two cups of the milk and put on the stove where it will get very hot, but not boil. Beat the egg and sugar until very light, add the chocolate and stir to smooth paste with the remaining half cup of milk, and cook to the consistency of soft jelly, stirring constantly. Pour in the heated milk and water, still stirring, and when well mixed, add vanilla and serve at once with a tablespoon of whipped cream on top of each cup.

PLAIN CHOCOLATE.

For each coffee cup of chocolate wanted allow one heaping tablespoon of grated chocolate, two thirds of a cup of fresh sweet *unskimmed* milk and one third of a cup of boiling water. Put the milk to scald, using a double boiler for the purpose, if convenient. Pour the boiling water on the chocolate, cook it a minute or two, stirring constantly. When the milk reaches the boiling point pour it over the cooked chocolate, stirring until well-mixed. Flavor delicately with vanilla, sweeten to taste, and serve with a bit of whipped cream to each cup.

SOFT GINGER BREAD.

4 cups sifted flour, 1 cup butter, 1 cup syrup, 1 cup buttermilk, 1 cup sugar, 2 eggs, 1 tablespoon cinnamon (pulverized), 1 tablespoon of ginger (pulverized), 1 teaspoon cloves (pulverized), ½ nutmeg grated, 2 teaspoons soda, 2 tablespoons warm water.

Cream the butter and sugar together, beat in the eggs, one at a time, and add [a] little flour, then syrup, then flour and milk, alternately, until all used, next, put in the spices, and last, the soda, which must first be dissolved in the warm water. Pour into a greased and papered shallow pan, and bake slowly with a moderate fire, as everything made with syrup is easily burned.

PRESSED CHICKEN.

1 grown chicken, ½ box gelatin, ½ cup cold water, 3 tablespoons melted butter, 1 tablespoon of white mustard seed, salt, red and black pepper to taste.

Dress and cut the chicken as for frying, using no salt. Put it into a stewpan, barely cover it with cold unsalted water, and boil slowly until it is so tender the meat will come to pieces when lifted with a fork. Drain off the water, which should measure about a cupful[,] and keep it hot, remove the bones from the chicken, and chop the meat fine, soak the gelatin in cold water until quite soft, then mix it with the hot chicken water, stirring until the gelatin is all melted. Pour this over the chicken, add the melted butter, sprinkle in the mustard seed, and season to taste with salt and pepper. Work the mass well with the hands, put it into a deep bowl or pan, set it in a cool place, (on ice, if convenient), and press for twelve hours. Slice thin and serve cold with nice mayonnaise.

BOILED LIVER.

2 pounds calf liver, butter the size of a large egg, 1 tablespoon melted lard, 1 tablespoon vinegar, 5 tablespoons tomato catsup, one scant teaspoon salt, black and cayenne pepper to taste.

Remove the skin and strings from the liver, chop lightly with a sharp knife, grease each side with the melted lard, and broil slowly until it is thoroughly done on ungreased bread hoe. Heat together the butter, vinegar, tomato catsup, salt and pepper, and pour over the liver while both are hot. Serve at once, as it is not so good when half cold.

DELICIOUS PLAIN OMELET.

6 eggs, 1 cup sweet milk, 1 tablespoon sifted flour, 2 tablespoons butter.

Scald half the milk, add the butter and let it come to a boil. Mix the flour with the remaining milk and a little salt, carefully beating out all lumps, then stir both mixtures well together, beat the eggs separately, add them, letting the whites come last. Pour into a very hot, well buttered frying pan, let it cook about four minutes or until [it] sets. Fold together and serve *at once*, on a hot flat dish.

BAKING POWDER.

½ pound cream tartar (best grade), ¼ pound soda, ¼ pound flour.

Sift all together *seven* times in a revolving sifter.

Table of Weights and Measures.

2 ordinary size tea cups of butter, weigh 1 pound.

2 ordinary size tea cups, level full, granulated sugar, weigh 1 pound.

4 ordinary size tea cups sifted flour, slightly heaped, weigh 1 pound.

1 quart sifted flour, slightly heaped, weighs 1 pound.

1 pint, level full, granulated sugar weighs 1 pound.

10 medium size unbroken eggs, weigh 1 pound.

1 ordinary size tea cup holds ½ pint.

2 level tablespoons liquid, weigh 1 ounce.

3 heaping tablespoons grated chocolate or pulverized spices, weigh 1 ounce.

Appendix

Holiday Recipes from the
Columbus Enquirer-Sun

In the fall of 1899, Emma Rylander Lane wrote a series of culinary articles for the *Columbus Enquirer-Sun*. She republished some of the recipes found in *Some Good Things to Eat* alongside new recipes for Thanksgiving and Christmas. While some of the recipes in the newspaper had additional instructions or commentary, only the titles of recipes included in her book are reproduced here. The recipes appear in order as they appeared in her newspaper series with the introductions. The only change is creating a new paragraph at the end of an ingredient list.

***

November 19, 1899

Cooking I regard as an art, indeed as one of the fine arts, but unfortunately it is a woefully neglected one. What sensible man would presume to take charge of a business, direct and manage his employees, without first mastering the business down to the smallest details. Yet we women, and we call ourselves sensible, too, marry and take upon ourselves the duties of a home, in utter ignorance, the majority of us, of the most important feature of the home—cooking and the kitchen. It is no wonder that we are at the mercy of our cooks. They soon discover our inability, and use, yes, and abuse us, too, at their pleasure. When I say that cooking is the most important branch of domestic work, I speak advisedly. Eat we must or die, and to the ignorant, inexperienced housekeeper, the three meals a day come with alarming regularity and rapidity. So much depends upon management in the kitchen—our husband's prosperity largely, and to a certain extent the health of the entire family. There is no greater drain upon a limited income than a wasteful, extravagant cook, and healthful, vigorous bodies we cannot expect, if we try to sustain ourselves upon unwholesome, badly cooked food. It is with much gratification that I note the adoption of cooking in the public schools of Columbus. In the training of our daughters too much importance cannot be attached to it, and what the mothers neglected, some willfully, some through their own inability, and others from necessity, it is well to have the city schools attend to. In continuing before the public as [an] authority on cooking, I shall endeavor to be plain, explicit and practical, and economy will be a special feature. Not the economy of doing without—but the economy of no waste or unnecessary outlay. As Thanksgiving and Christmas are near at hand, these recipes are selected with a view to preparing beforehand, such things as will be most generally used upon those occasions, and can be kept indefinitely, without danger of spoiling. Some of them are taken from my cook book, "Some Good Things to Eat," and others are given to the public for the first time. All have been tested and no failure will result if directions are closely and intelligently followed. Each housewife can use only such recipes as are best suited to her means, and to the taste of her family.

BROWN FRUIT CAKE.

BLACK FRUIT CAKE.

WHITE FRUIT CAKE.

One pound granulated sugar, 1 pound flour, ½ pound butter, 1 teaspoon baking powder, ½ cup alcohol, mixed with ¼ cup cold water, 1 lemon (juice only), 12 egg whites, 1 pound seeded raisins, 1 pound citron, 1 pound shelled almonds, 1 pound crystalized pineapple, 1 pound dried figs.

Prepare the pans and fruits, as directed in Brown Fruit Cake, with this difference: without washing, cut the pineapple into small bits, and the same for the figs, leaving out the stems. To make the batter, cream butter with half the sugar, adding the lemon juice by degrees. Break the eggs and thoroughly beat the yolks and put them aside to make into mayonnaise while the cake is cooking. Whip the whites until stiff, add to them remaining sugar, and beat until it is dissolved; then mix with the creamed butter. Last, fold in the flour, after first sifting it three times with the baking powder. Put in the fruits and almonds, a little of each, stir carefully, add more, stir again, and so on until all are put in; then add the alcohol. The batter will be very stiff and hard, but the cake, when properly baked, is soft and tender, very full of fruit and the most delicate and finely flavored of all fruit cakes. It requires slow, careful baking, and while hot should be turned upside down, moistened with white wine and iced.

GOLDEN WEDDING FRUIT CAKE.

One pound sifted flour, 1 pound granulated sugar, ¾ pound butter, 1 heaping teaspoon baking powder, 1 pound shelled almonds, 1 pound crystalized pineapple, 1 pound crystalized cherries, 1 pound citron, 1/3 cup alcohol, mixed with 1 tablespoon cold water. Mix the batter as directed in Brown Fruit Cake. Prepare the pans and fruits, then put together, bake and ice, the same as White Fruit Cake.

MAYONNAISE.

MINCE MEAT.

Five pounds lean tender beef, 3 pounds butter, 4 pounds seeded and clipped raisins, 4 pounds cleaned currants, 1 pound finely cut citron, 4 quarts crisp, chopped apples (measured after cutting), 2 ounces pulverized cinnamon, 1 ounce pulverized cloves, 1 ounce ground ginger, 4 grated nutmegs, juice and grated yellow rind of 2 lemons, 2 pounds sugar, 1 teaspoon black pepper, 1 quart cider, or 1 pint each vinegar and water, 1 quart syrup.

Cover the beef with cold water, stew gently until very tender, salt to taste, cut fine and mix it thoroughly with the prepared fruits, spices, lemons and pepper. Into a granite, iron or porcelain kettle, put the cider, syrup and butter, let them come to a boil and while hot stir well into the fruits and meat. If a rich, highly seasoned mince meat is desired, add to it 1 pint of alcohol, or 1 ½ pints whiskey. When quite cold, pack into stone or glass jars, cover ½ of an inch in syrup, and set away in a cool place. This makes a nice supply, and keeps well.

CRANBERRY JELLY.

Pick and wash the cranberries, cover them well with cold water, and boil gently until they are quite tender. Strain through a wire sieve, add an equal quantity of granulated sugar, return to the fire and boil rapidly, until it jellies.

November 26, 1899

Thanksgiving all should try to celebrate, even if some sacrifices have to be made in order to do so. The day should be one of feasting and merrymaking, freedom from care and business, and a day of recreation and rest as well. We should remember, all of us, that we have much to be thankful for, whether or not we realize or appreciate it. Our style of entertaining on that day should be suited to our means first and next to the taste of our families, and such guests as may honor us with their presence. In making preparations for our feast we should have ready beforehand such dishes as can be kept without detriment to their good qualities, leaving us some time to give to our friends and family, also saving so much unnecessary hurry and confusion. From the recipes given below a menu can be selected, simple or elaborate, as the number of guests and means of the hostess demand, keeping in mind the fact that the feast is hardly perfect without the time-honored turkey, with his trimmings of cranberry jelly, supplemented with mince pie or plum pudding and sauce.

OYSTER SOUP.

To the quantity of oysters used, allow an equal portion of fresh, sweet milk with half the quantity of boiling water. First pour the hot water into a deep vessel, adding the oysters in their liquor. Place over a hot fire, and when it comes to a good boil, add the milk. Season generously with butter, adding salt and black pepper to taste. Just as the soup reaches the boiling point, without allowing it to boil, pour it over heated oysters crackers, taste, governing the quantity, and serve quite hot.

ROAST TURKEY.

The turkey should be killed, dressed, well rubbed, inside and out, with salt and black pepper, and kept in a cold place, at least two days and nights. Before cooking, wash thoroughly with warm water and rub inside and out with cold lard or butter. Put into a baking pan with the giblets (liver and gizzard) in not more than 1 ½ inches cold water and place in a hot stove on the bottom rack. As soon as the juices begin to run out, baste every ten minutes or oftener, with the water in the pan, turning the turkey from side to side, as it browns. When it is perfectly tender, without being cooked to pieces, remove from the fire. A rich dressing is made by putting into the gravy a quart of oysters drained from their liquor and cooked a few minutes, adding a very little hot water, if the gravy has cooked down too low. Another nice dressing, not so expensive, is made by grating cold breads of all sorts, biscuit, light bread, muffins, etc. etc., and seasoning with a little lard, some melted butter, finely chopped onions, and black pepper, adding hot water if it seems too dry. Mix all thoroughly and cook on top of the stove until done, thinning frequently. Cut giblets into remaining gravy, thicken with browned flour, and serve hot. Only the larger slices of the turkey should be served, leaving the bones. Where economy is considered, and it is a duty of most households, the bits of meat should be carefully removed from the bones and used in hash or croquettes. The bones should be cracked, generously covered with hot water, and boiled gently [for] six or more hours. This liquor, or stock, should be strained through a wire sieve, made into a soup, seasoning with butter, sweet milk, salt and black pepper to taste, poured over heated oyster crackers and served hot. This is a rich and most delicious soup, if properly made.

COLD SLICED PORK.

Select a pork ham, one from a pig not overfat is best. Rub well with salt, black and cayenne pepper, and keep in a cold place, one or more days. Wash well, cover with water and boil gently but steadily, keeping it covered until tender. Remove from the liquor and when quite cold, cut into [thin] slices and serve with mayonnaise dressing, the recipe for which was given in the *Enquirer Sun* of November 19. The liquor in which the ham was cooked should be poured into a bowl, set aside, and when cold the grease carefully skimmed off and kept for seasoning or frying purposes. The stock should be saved and used for gravies and soups.

CRAB SALAD.

EGG SALAD.

CANDIED SWEET POTATOES.

First bake the potatoes, and peel while hot, or cold ones can be used if preferable. Slice them moderately thin and fill a buttered pie pan with alternate layers of the sliced potatoes, a liberal sprinkling of sugar and plenty of butter. Let the top layer be well covered with sugar and butter, set in a hot oven and brown. Use no water, but 2 or 3 tablespoons of good wine, put in just before cooking, is quite an addition. Serve hot.

CREAMED IRISH POTATOES.

First peel the potatoes with a sharp knife, wash in cold water, cover well with boiling water—no salt. Cook them with the vessel covered, until tender, then drain off the water, and put on the back of the stove, where they will steam a few minutes until dry. Mash them with a silver fork or potato masher, until entirely free from lumps. While hot, season with butter, black pepper and salt to taste. Cream into them heated sweet milk or cream, the quantity depending on how many potatoes are used. Last, stir in the well whipped whites of one or more eggs, putting them in before the potatoes are allowed to cool. Serve hot.

CRISP DINNER BISCUIT.

MINCE PIES.

Pastry for mince pies should be rich and crisp, rather than light and delicate, as the mince meat is so heavy and juicy. For making the pastry, use 1 quart unsifted flour, 1 heaping teaspoon baking powder, 1 heaping teaspoon salt, 1 cup cold, stiff lard, 1 cup ice water. Sift flour and baking powder twice together, rub lard into it with a spoon, dissolve salt in the water and mix to a stiff dough, still using the spoon and working in more flour if needed. Do not put the hands into the dough, or try to smooth it. Take from the mass about what is wanted to line one pan, roll to about 1/8 of an inch thickness, being careful not to stretch it. Fill nearly to the top with "mince meat," the recipe for which was given in the *Enquirer Sun* of Nov. 19. Roll out the top crust and before putting it on wet the edges of the undercrust with soft, uncooked flour paste. After putting on the top crust, press the edges firmly together; cut away the overhanging sides, stick with a fork, and bake slowly to a delicate brown. There should be sufficient pastry for two pies, provided the pans used are not too large. These pies should be made a day or more before needed, slipped into granite plates as soon as baked and served cold.

MACAROON CREAM.

***

December 3, 1899

To all housekeepers the question of "what shall I have for dessert" is at times a most annoying one. The matter becomes really serious when each day's dinner demands a dessert. Where it can be made the evening before—possible while supper is being prepared—no small amount of worry and often valuable time is saved. Heavy, elaborate dinners should be followed by dainty, light desserts, and what is termed "short dinners" call for something richer and more substantial than "moonshine sweets." Then comes the time for the great American pie. No article of cooked food in this country is more universally used, or more generally abused than this same "pie." When we eat a sure enough good one, and find it "food for the gods," we wish it was even more used. When a bad one (and they are many) is put before us, we join the army of abusers and wonder how even a self-respecting pig could eat such a mess. After all, it does not require a large amount of skill to make a good pie— only a little judgement, a careful following of recipes, good materials always and some experience, of course. In most open pies and custards the crusts and fillings should be cooked separately, each allowed to cool, and just before serving put together. If required hot, they can be placed in the stove and reheated without detriment to their good qualities. All of the recipes given this week are for desserts, and some of them are published in obedience to requests. Any information or recipe wanted I will take pleasure in furnishing through this column, but will give no more recipes verbally or by letter.

VERY LIGHT DELICATE PASTRY.

PLAIN CRISP PASTRY.

APPLE CUSTARD.

Six apples, 1 tea cup sweet milk, 3 eggs, 1 heaping tablespoon butter, 1 scant tablespoon corn starch or flour, 2 cups sugar.

Peel the apples and cut them into small pieces, removing the cores. (If the apples are sound the cores and peeling will make a nice mold of jelly.) Cover the apples with boiling water, put in 1 ½ cups of sugar and cook on top of the stove until perfectly done, stirring frequently and mashing to a pulp. Wet the corn starch with a little of the milk, stir it into the apples, then drop in the butter. Separate the eggs, beating the yolks well, mix with them the remaining milk, add to the apples and cook until thick and pasty, stirring constantly. When cold, fill pastry shells, cover with a meringue made by beating the egg whites until stiff, then stirring into them the leftover sugar— ½ cup. Sprinkle a little dry sugar and grate a bit of nutmeg over the top. Return to the stove and brown, remembering that the fire must not be very hot, as a meringue is easily burned. This will fill two medium sized shells.

DRIED APPLE CUSTARD.

Carefully pick the apples, pour boiling water over them, then wash in cold water. Cover them well with boiling water, cook until quite tender, then press through a wire sieve or potato masher. To 3 cups of the apples put 1 ½ cups sugar, 1 heaping tablespoon butter, 1 cup sweet milk, and yolks of 3 eggs well beaten. Cook all together on top of the stove, stirring constantly. When thick, take from the fire, cool and flavor with vanilla. Fill pastry shells, cover with a meringue made of the 3 egg whites and ½ cup sugar, and brown. Sufficient for two custards.

SWEET POTATO CUSTARD.

Peel the potatoes, cut them into thin slices, wash, cover with boiling water, and cook until quite soft. Drain off the water and wash until perfectly free from lumps and quite smooth. To 3 cups of the mashed potato put 2 heaping tablespoons butter, 1 cup sugar, juice and grated rind of 1 lemon, yolks of 4 eggs, well beaten, and 2 cups fresh buttermilk, first beating into it 1 rounded teaspoon soda. Cook a few minutes on top of the stove, stirring constantly. Fill pastry shells, cover with a meringue made of the 4 whites and ¾ cup sugar and brown. This makes 3 custards.

SLICED POTATO PIE.

Wash the potatoes and boil them in their jackets. When not quite done, take them from the fire, peel, slice thin and thoroughly cool. Line deep pie pans with plain crisp pastry, and fill with layers of the sliced potato, thickly sprinkled with sugar and generous bits of butter. Let the top layer be sugar and butter, then fill the pan nearly full with a mixture of half each cold water and wine, or vinegar. Put strips of the pastry across the top and bake slowly until done.

SLICED APPLE PIE.

Make the same as sliced potato pie, except slice the apples raw and add a little grated nutmeg to the top.

PRUNE SPONGE.

One quart flour sifted 3 times with 2 heaping teaspoons baking powder. Pour into this 1 pint sweet milk and beat until smooth and free from lumps, adding 1 tablespoon melted butter. Separate 4 eggs and beat the yolks one at a time into the batter. Last, stir in the cold whipped whites, and bake in jet pie pans. When done, put together as you would a layer cake, turning each layer upside down, buttering it generously, sprinkling with sugar, and spreading thickly with stewed and sweetened prunes. Serve with the following, or any prepared sauce: 1 ½ cups sugar, 1 tablespoon butter, ½ cup water, ½ cup wine, boiled together without stirring until the consistency of syrup. While steaming hot, pour over a well beaten egg, stirring rapidly to prevent lumping. Serve both the sponge and the sauce hot. When it is not convenient to use sweet milk, fresh buttermilk can be substituted, using the same quantity, but beating into it 1 teaspoon soda, and using in the flour half the amount of baking powder. For the layers, any stewed fruit will answer.

FRUIT PUDDING.

One quart sweet milk, yolks of 6 eggs, 4 tablespoons flour, or corn starch, 1 cup sugar, 1 tablespoon butter.

Beat the egg yolks and sugar until perfectly light, stir the flour into them, add the milk and boil together until very thick, putting in the butter after it begins to boil, stirring constantly. While still hot, flavor delicately with lemon, put into a buttered pudding dish, sprinkling in ½ cup raisins, seeded and clipped, and ¼ pound crystalized pineapple, cut into bits. Cover with a meringue made of the egg whites, beaten stiff with 6 table-spoons sugar, and bake to a delicate brown.

COCONUT PUDDING.

Three cups grated coconut, 3 cups sugar, 1 cup sweet milk, 3 eggs, 3 tablespoons butter.

Beat eggs and sugar until light, stir in coconut and sweet milk, add butter, first melting it, pour into a buttered pudding dish and serve hot or cold.

Acknowledgments

My experience in southwestern Georgia exceeded my expectations. In 2015, faced with a choice between three jobs—a one-year job in Montana, a one-year job in Washington, DC, and a six-month job at Andersonville National Historic Site—I took the one closest to Amanda, my girlfriend and future wife. But that was not the only factor. I also had no furniture. Roger Pickenpaugh, an historian from Ohio whom I had befriended two years before, said that his sister, Jill Stuckey, could rent me a furnished room in Plains. As often is the case, Amanda's advice was eerily prescient. "Move to Plains, become friends with Jimmy Carter, and use his connections to get the next job," she said. "People have made careers on less." While that is not exactly how it happened, it is fair to say that it was the network of Jimmy and Rosalynn Carter's friends, beginning with Roger and Jill, who supported my postdoctoral attempts to carve out a career in both academic and public history. Jill even let me live in what locals call the Jimmy Carter "conception room" (a long story for another time).

Plains quickly felt like home. For years, Jill's dining room and kitchen were the places to be on a Friday and Saturday night. Often present were not only President Carter and Rosalynn Carter, but also the regulars from town and the constant visitors from out of town. For fear of leaving out specific names, let me just say you know who you are, and please know how important those times were to me. The "haunted house" was often a topic of conversation and a place to visit after the sun went down. With the help of Patrick Rios, those conversations spun off into local history research that ended, for a time, when we learned the house was already listed in the National Register of Historic Places. This was years before I learned the name Emma Rylander, though. Credit for that connection—the link between the house and the family that launched my search for an original copy of *Some Good Things to Eat*—belongs to Michele Dunn.

When the COVID-19 pandemic prevented me from traveling to see a rare copy of the cookbook, Kyle Munroe photographed pages for me. I was impressed with the text, but I still only envisioned a short article about the Lane cake. Then serendipity intervened. Marsha Luttrell, who I worked with on *Ossabaw Island, A Sense of Place* (2016), saw a social media post about the cookbook and asked if I was interested in editing it for Mercer University Press. At Marsha's suggestion and the encouragement of series editor Fred Sauceman, the pieces came into place. Lee Kinnamon gave up many hours mulling the significance of the Rylander family and the Lane cake. Keith Bohannon shared his invaluable notes on Maj. Emory Rylander. Kathy Shoemaker, of Emory University, scanned pages of Emory Rylander's correspondence. Jennifer Griffin offered clear editorial suggestions in the later stages. Rebecca Beasley, on short notice, shared her introduction to the 1976 reprint and the local traditions of the Lane cake. Most of my projects, big and small, require the help of many people. This one was no different.

My household and my extended family have supported this project in myriad ways. My mother, Paula Frank, and my mother-in-law, Beverly Noll, offered helpful suggestions early on in the project. Amanda, who came from Charleston to join me in southwest Georgia, continues to show remarkable patience for projects that can, at times, distract me. This was also the first big project since the birth of our daughter, Evelyn. Born during the pandemic, she and I drove to Alabama in the spring of 2022 to see what we could learn about the Lane cake in Clayton. While having her first experience at a diner, including her first Coca-Cola, hamburger, and french fries, may not have been adequate compensation for a four-hour, round-trip car ride, it was an adventure I will never forget. It is in the spirit of adventure and valuing mysteries large and small that I dedicate this project to her.

Index

Index